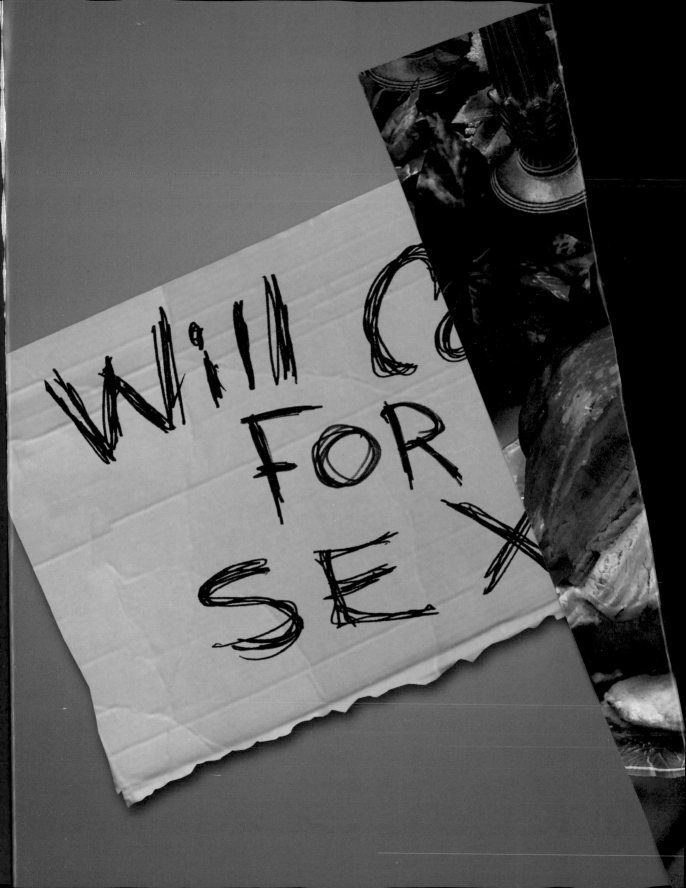

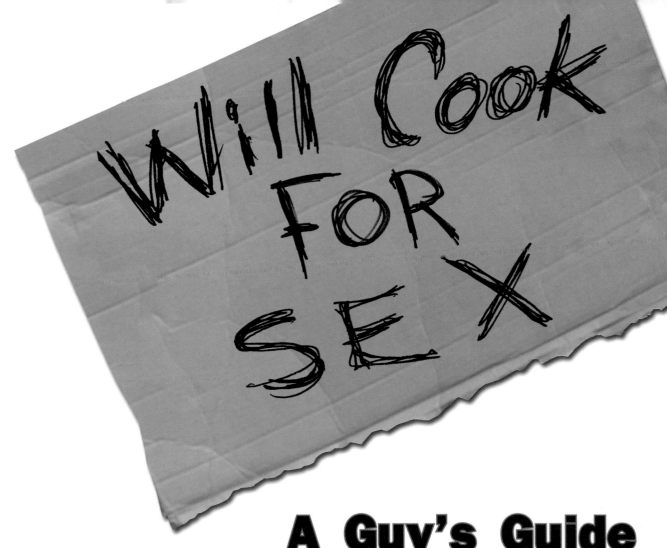

A Guy's Guide to Cooking

Rocky Fino

STEPHENS
PRESS, LLC

A STEPHENS MEDIA COMPANY

LAS VEGAS, NEVADA

Editor: Heidi Knapp Rinella
Photographer: Fred Armitage, Visual Impact
Creative Direction/Design: Chris Wheeler
Cover Model: Monika Orban

ISBN-10: 1-932173-51-X
ISBN-13: 9781-932173-512

CIP Data Available

STEPHENS
PRESS, LLC

A STEPHENS MEDIA COMPANY
P.O. BOX 1600, LAS VEGAS, NEVADA 89125-1600
TEL 702.387.5260 • FAX 702.387.2997
www.stephenspress.com

Printed in Hong Kong

*Here's to good food, fine wine...
and wherever that may lead!*

P

To all my friends and family whom
I have had the fortune of sharing good food,
good booze and great laughs.

troglodyte \TROG-luh-dyt\, noun:

1. A member of a primitive people dwelling in caves, dens, or holes; cavemanlike.

"I enjoyed talking about this crazy book — which despite its sometimes troglodyte view of dating — has some great recipes and good advice for guys who want to cook gourmet meals for their dates, but don't know how to get started."

— Jaqueline Church Simonds, Beagle Bay Books

Contents

A Foreword from the Author's Father

As a father you try to teach your kids some skills, initially to get them out of the nest and hopefully to get them through life. Coax them to get an education, teach them responsibilities like how to read the daily racing form…things that will take them places.

Well, Rocky got the education, but never quite grasped the corporate structure. He adjusted quite well to the three-martini lunch, however. I should've known since from early on he had one hell of an appetite and passion for food. When he was young, I taught him some of the basics. Since then, he and I have continued to expand our techniques and have had some great meals along the way.

He's taken those skills and produced what I consider something new, a fun and purposeful reason to cook. This book provides the tools using step-by-step photography for any novice to enter the kitchen and impress his date with elegant yet simple dishes.

I've been cooking for a long time, and I can understand looking at most cookbooks that a newcomer can get discouraged. Ingredients are not recognized, names are different, and recipes are difficult to follow. Rarely will they turn out to look or taste anything like restaurant presentation shown in the book. There are tricks and subtleties to cooking that may take years to understand. Rocky's left the tricks out and the recipes work the first time. Using limited ingredients found in most locales, gourmet results are obtained.

Give it at try. I'm certain your date will be impressed, and you'll enjoy doing it. I always kidded him, claiming "I never knew I liked sex until I tried it!" I guess he took me serious.

— The Old Man

(Fred)

Introduction

My father taught me that a man can really get respect — not to mention the "luck" any guy needs with women — if he knows how to cook.

The Old Man has cooked elegant meals for family and friends since I was a kid. He was the one who first told me, "Enough money can buy most pleasures in life, but creating them adds a new dimension. In fact, it's never a waste of time to cook for just one or two people." He'd say, "Why waste an opportunity? You've only got so many meals in your life, and they should not all taste the same."

He also admitted that since I didn't get Paul Newman looks from him, he needed to give me something else to help with the ladies.

When I was younger, we'd often work together in the kitchen preparing more than one dinner at a time, simply to experiment with flavors. We've been the designated cooks on many family trips through the years; and when we weren't cooking, we'd dine at elegant restaurants so we could compare our creations with those of the pros. Over time I learned what my father meant when he said, "There's a hell of a lot more to cooking than just heat." Cooking was magic, and I came to love it, whether it was with family, friends — or a woman I wanted to impress.

The way I see it, a way to a man's heart is through his zipper. The way to a woman's heart is through her stomach.

My old man never told me how to get laid, but he did train me how to cook. And after many years of defeat suffered while trying to go toe-to-toe in the ring of the pick-up scene, I finally realized the value of that skill.

If you've gained the reputation of a porn star (size does matter, after all) and/or have the animal magnetism to lure women with a smile and a wink, I envy you.

But the rest of us need a more strategic approach. A woman's expectations of men's abilities are even lower than you'd think. Your attempt alone will impress her more than buying her dinner, and if it's good, you're bound to move up in the rankings.

The way I see it, a way to a man's heart is through his zipper. The way to a woman's heart is through her stomach.

The first time I cooked for a woman, I was young, the meal was marginal, and she was too naïve to know any better.

I got lucky!

I never questioned the power of food again.

I've gotten older, the women are getting wiser, and their expectations just keep rising. Fortunately, I've continued to work on my game. For those who haven't — or have no idea what game I'm talking about — here's the book to help you.

The Cook

A woman once said to me, "You cook and clean? You must be gay!"

No. Many straight — and manly — guys do cook, and believe me, women love them.

Fewer women cook today, and we know why: They're busy. Many of the women I know work harder than I do and consider the kitchen mainly a storage unit for the Starbucks travel mugs that keep them flying through their day. They offer to take us out and pick up the tab or at least go dutch — anything to avoid adding meal preparation to their busy days. You don't have to say "no" if she's buying, but when it's time to return the favor, charming her from your kitchen (or hers) will separate you from the herd. You're The Straight Guy Who Cooks.

She remembers someone cooking for her when she was a kid, and childhood memories are powerful. People remember a great hook-up, a great round, and a great meal. If you're not so good at the first two, the latter is a good cover.

A woman once said to me, "You cook and clean? You must be gay!" No.

For those of you who've never cooked before, I've kept this book simple — the way I'd have liked it when I was starting out. You'll find my easy but time-tested recipes will win the hearts of women, family and friends. And they're accompanied by step-by-step photos to keep things clear.

Once you've mastered the basics, you can start experimenting, as my dad and I did. Eventually you'll be able to do it without looking at the book. Imagine the look in her eye when you do.

In the meantime, if you've got a date and want to get lucky, just follow the steps in this book.

What You Need
Basic Equipment

Essential equipment:

- **3 non-stick pans**
- **Pots – small to large**
- **Tongs**
- **A sharp knife**
- **A spatula**
- **2 large spoons (one slotted – the kind with holes)**
- **A cutting board**
- **A measuring cup**
- **Measuring spoons**
- **Mixing bowls**
- **A blender**
- **An apron**
- **Cookie Sheet**
- **Roasting Pan**
- **Ramekins (small baking bowl)**
- **A corkscrew**

Many cookbooks assume the reader has a completely outfitted kitchen. When it comes to guys, that's a stupid assumption. Outside of an ESPN feed, nothing should be assumed. A completely outfitted kitchen isn't necessary, anyway. The equipment you need to turn yourself into a cook is minimal and shouldn't cost more than a couple of hundred bucks. It's worth it.

You'll need non-stick skillets in various sizes, and you can buy them as a set. Even cheap ones will do. But any tool that touches the inside of the pan should be plastic or wood, because metal will scratch the finish. Then again, if you buy cheap non-stick pans, and you scratch them, you can buy new ones.

As for the tongs, spring-loaded ones work best.

And get an apron. If you don't, you're going to be doing a lot of laundry, because if nothing else, you'll wipe your hands on your jeans without knowing it. Besides, an apron on a guy — miracle that it is — is a turn-on for many women.

The corkscrew is also essential. There is more to entertaining — and scoring — than cooking.

Optional equipment:
- Extra pans
- Additional knives
- A roasting rack
- A deep pot
- Whisk
- Mallet (wood or steel)
- Corkscrews, corkscrews, and more corkscrews

If you've got a patio, porch or yard, you should have a grill. But if you can't cook outdoors at your place, don't worry about it.

Though the food can stand on its own, decorative plates and serving dishes will make it look classy, and that's a turn-on, too.

As for the corkscrews, my old man always says, "corkscrews are like car keys — you're never sure where you left them." Always have extras.

Basic Ingredients

After the equipment, you'll want to stock your kitchen with some basic ingredients, which you'll need for almost every recipe in the book.

I'm Italian and was bottle-fed olive oil as a baby. Never run out of olive oil. And don't buy any exotic spices. You don't need them at this stage, and can make deadly mistakes with them.

Essential ingredients:

- Olive oil
- Salt
- Pepper
- Butter
- Cayenne pepper
- White wine vinegar
- Flour

If your kitchen's ready, you're ready. Now tell her you're going to cook and watch what happens.

This is my last bit of advice before you take the field. You've heard it said before, "In real estate…it's location, location, location." You can build a beautiful home, but if you don't start in the right neighborhood, you won't get the results you're looking for. You need to start with a good location.

I say, "In cooking…it's ingredients, ingredients, ingredients." If you take the time to shop for fresh, quality ingredients, then you're 'rounding second and headed for third' before heating up your first pan. A little extra concentration while shopping will increase the probabilities of success, tenfold.

Remember, we're dealing with women. Outside of jewelry, there are no guarantees. We're working on increasing your chances.

The Date

I'm always excited about a dinner date, especially with a woman.

For starters, I like to hang out in the kitchen. Offering to cook enables me to attend to some duties in the kitchen while at the same time hosting. This need for action prevents those "dead air" moments that occur from the downtimes in the conversation. In addition to that, it creates conversation. I could talk about a meal for hours – although I don't recommend you do that.

The first time that you offer to cook for her, her expectations of your talents are presumably low. Let's surprise her with a little romance. It's simple: Some good food, a little ambience, and some attentive listening will do the trick.

First things first: Get the Chardonnay chilling. I must take a moment at this point to emphasize the importance of the wine. Every recipe in this book — whether it is for breakfast, lunch, dinner or dessert — can be enhanced by a bottle of good wine. Do some research (like checking the ratings at the wine shop, or asking for a recommendation). The wine doesn't need to be expensive, but like the food, it needs to be good. A good meal with bad wine is no different than driving downfield, getting into the red zone, and giving up the ball without a score. You'll get beat in the end.

Now me, I wear an apron. I'm convinced that wearing an apron is a turn-on for women. It's one of those moves that give the impression that you're domesticated, and the allure of domestication can be irresistible.

Next, get the table set before she arrives, because first impressions are lasting ones. Don't spare the candles. Candlelight is not a cliché: It creates an ambience that adds to the presentation. You want to avoid harsh direct lighting when you can, and candlelight offers the soft lighting that will accentuate the meal and filter your appearance at the same time. It's a win-win.

This is your first dinner date at your place. I recommend that you don't put all of your eggs in one basket and attempt to time four or five dishes at once, which can be overwhelming and definitely not as much fun. Set it up so you can delight her with a variety of what you know, and allow for time between courses so you can enjoy it together. You don't want her eating alone as you are bouncing in and out of your chair for the kitchen.

And there's another thing: When I've got to rush in the kitchen, I start sweating. The next thing I know, beads of sweat are dripping off of my nose, and I am wiping my forehead with the kitchen towel — not exactly a turn-on. So be prepared and take your time. Remember, unlike at a restaurant where management is hoping you'll finish quickly so they can turn the table, you're on your home court. You have all night. A great meal, fine wine, candlelight: We're not trying to reinvent the wheel here. This is a proven method of success.

WARNING– A cute move with beer and pizza works ONLY if you're Ben Affleck.

WARNING — A cute move with beer and pizza works ONLY if you're Ben Affleck. If you have that kind of confidence in your game, great; but, remember, you're not Ben Affleck and the scene was scripted, anyway.

In addition to avoiding the beer and pizza trick, try to minimize the barbecue influence on the meal. There are some grilling requirements throughout this book, but they're not to be confused with the misconception that grilling is the man's sole cooking domain. Meat charred over a fire — which is Item 2 on The List of Three Standards That a Man Knows How to Cook — will not impress her.

I'm giving you what I believe is a fail-safe program for the first three occasions you will cook for her, along with some additional recommendations for occasions during the ensuing relationship.

There are no guarantees in the world of dating, and plenty of things can go wrong. With all of the variables involved you're capable of screwing up something on your own, but the meals will not be your problem. Food presented in this fashion should provide you a cushion for your inevitable mistakes. Good luck!

The First Pitch

You've got the wine chilling for dinner, but she might want to start with a cocktail. Not a problem. "Never eat on an empty stomach," the old man always says.

A martini, perhaps? Martinis come in a multitude of flavors and colors these days, but be careful. A more seasoned man once told me, "One martini is a good date. Two martinis is a great date. Three martinis and the date is over." Of course, if your date can handle three martinis, skip dinner and move to Chapter 2, "The Morning After."

A light, refreshing starter might be a Ruumo. A variation of the classic Rum and Coke, this cocktail originated in the Mexican state of Campeche, so it's also called a "Campecheno." It's simple, but you've got to use real Coke or Pepsi. "Diet" will kill it.

Ruumo	*Ruumo "Up On its Feet!"*
1/3 Coke	¼ Coke
1/3 Club soda	¼ Club soda
1/3 Rum	½ Rum
Lime	Lime

Serve over ice.

The club soda tempers the overbearing Coke and lets the taste of the rum come through. Be sure to use good rum. While she's enjoying her drink, you get the meal started.

The Show

It's your first time — and it's your show. She'll be on her best behavior, wondering what's going to happen, and you're in charge. First impressions matter. You'll want to start with a bang, and the following menu guarantees you will.

First Course

Power Play Pucks

She won't be expecting this, and it will make a great first impression. The beauty of this dish is that after your first try you'll be able to make it in 10 to 15 minutes. The tricky part is finding the giant scallops. Try a good fish market, or even ask at the fish counter of your local supermarket; they may be able to order them for you.

Second course

Hidden Greens

Same gig: It's stylish and she's not expecting it. It's a sweet and nutty combination of pears, almonds and blue cheese in a raspberry vinaigrette. Presentation is crucial, so take the time to set it up right.

Third course

Red Zone Chops

She's expecting you to use the grill at some point, and you certainly don't want to disappoint her. But this is no Fourth of July burger, and she'll be impressed. The pepper and rosemary go well with the lamb chop, providing her with a first-class entree.

These make a great lineup, but first find out if she is allergic to anything or simply doesn't like seafood or lamb. If she is (or doesn't), use a substitution from the recipes, or choose a different selection entirely. Always accommodate a guest — especially a female one. But if she doesn't like any of these courses, you may want to consider cutting your losses. You can't cook for her if she won't let you.

If you're a little nervous or self-conscious, this menu will help, because you can prepare quite a bit of it in advance. This will also let you focus more on conversation — something any woman appreciates. Also be sure to space the courses out for a leisurely and full evening. Keep the portions small. It's the first date; no matter how small the portion is, she probably won't finish it. That's fine, because this menu makes great leftovers.

If you've been together for a while but have never cooked for her, approach the evening as if it were your first date. That kind of attention to detail — and to her — always pays off.

My old man taught me a lot, but he didn't teach me to be a pastry baker. Nothing's simple in that kind of baking. If the first three courses have gone well, of course you'll want to give her dessert. Keep is simple: Fruit and cheese are classy and never fail. Neither does chocolate. Besides, if she's still reveling in memories of the dinner, why hit her with a carb-loaded dessert that weighs more than the first three courses? A simple finish allows for a smooth transition from the kitchen. A nice glass of Cabernet with some Godiva chocolate says, "Life is good."

Keep the portions small. It's the first date; no matter how small the portion is, she probably won't finish it.

WARNING:
If your woman doesn't like chocolate (the most sensuous dessert ingredient there is), she may not be the woman for you.

POWER PLAY PUCKS

INGREDIENTS

Mango	1
Scallops	6 large
Parsley	2 sprigs
Milk	3 tablespoons
Cayenne pepper	Dash
Olive oil	½ teaspoon

Step one

- Peel and slice the mango. Discard the seed and skin.
- Add mango, splash of milk and dash of cayenne pepper to blender and puree the mixture.
- Use cayenne pepper sparingly to taste. It gives a great spicy taste but too much will make the puree unpalatable.

Note

The amount of milk is flexible, the more you use, the thinner the sauce. Too thin will roll all over the plate. You want the consistency of thick gravy. It is better to put less. You can always add but you can't take away.

Step two

- Preheat medium size non-stick pan, and add a few drops of olive oil
- Brown scallops on both sides over medium/high heat
- Cooking time for the scallops is about 2-3 minutes on each side.

Using very little olive oil with a non-stick pan gives a brown glaze look, as the water evaporates from the scallops.

Step three

- Place mango puree on plate — Best at room temperature
- Add the scallops on top of the puree
- Garnish with parsley

Serves 2

Hint
Scallops are done when the center is still clear and appears raw. They will be very tender and can be cut with a fork. If overcooked, they become rubbery and tough.

25

HIDDEN GREENS

INGREDIENTS

Pear	½
Baby greens	4 oz.
Crumbled blue cheese	2 oz. (¼ cup)
Raspberries	4 oz.
Almonds (sliced or slivered)	2 oz. (¼ cup)

Raspberry Vinaigrette:

Olive oil	2 tablespoons
White wine vinegar	1 tablespoons
Raspberries (mashed)	2 tablespoons

Step one

- Cut pear into 3/8" squares or rectangles

Step two

Prepare raspberry vinaigrette

- In a small cup mix 2 tablespoons of olive oil, 1 tablespoon of white wine vinegar and 2 tablespoons mashed raspberries

Step three

- In a salad bowl toss ingredients
- Add raspberry vinaigrette to bowl and toss just before serving
- Garnish with remaining raspberries and serve

Serves 2

RED ZONE CHOPS

HOW TO MAKE RED ZONE CHOPS

INGREDIENTS

Lamb chops..........................4
Cracked pepper............2 tablespoons
Rosemary.....................4 stems

Step one

- Remove rosemary leaves from stem
- Chop leaves finely

Step two

- Trim fat from lamb chops (optional)
- Sprinkle pepper on both sides of lamb chops
- Generously add rosemary on top of pepper and pat lightly with hand to help adhere to chops

Note

Steps 1 and 2 can be completed in advance. Simply cover with plastic wrap and refrigerate until time to cook.

I recommend rare to medium rare, but cook to your guest's taste.

Step three

- Pre-heat grill on high
- Place chops on grill
- Approximately 2 – 3 minutes per side

Step four

- Place chops on plate, garnish with parsley

Variation

- Use 2 veal chops in place of 4 lamb chops

Serves 2

The Swing Date

The fact that she's now said "yes" to a second date means this book worked, but success is a two-edged sword. You did good. Your cooking worked. But now you need to prove that you're not a One Meal Wonder. She's still debating what other men — and cooks, if any — might be out there. She may be giving you a second chance simply for lack of a better offer, so what happens on the second date is crucial. That's why I call it "The Swing Date."

You can offer her chocolate again, unless she finished your chocolate reserves on the first date.

The second date is your chance to show her you're not just a cook, but a human being. Toward this goal, the menu for the second date drops a course and lets you spend more time with her. There is, after all — painful as it is to admit — more to life than food, and you've got to show her you understand this.

Ambience is still essential, soft lighting a must. And again, prep the salad in advance so you have fewer things to think about and can really focus on her.

First course

Greyhound Pecan Salad

This salad contains a more common type of lettuce than "Hidden Greens" did, but it combines grapefruit slices and walnuts for a solid first course.

NOTE: When you prepare a salad in advance, keep the lettuce cold and in the crisper until the last minute to prevent wilting, and never add the dressing until it's time to serve.

Second course

Seahawk Pasta

You'll want to prepare this one in front of her, since she'll enjoy that. Pastas require a little concentration, but not enough to stress over. Boil the pasta until it's "al dente" — neither crunchy nor overcooked. The best way to test — and you can test more than once, but don't get carried away — is to taste a noodle or two. You also don't want the sauce to sit in the pan too long, so time the pasta according to the instructions on the box or bag. She does expect you to know how to cook spaghetti by adding noodles to boiling water and using sauce from a jar (Item 3 on The list of Three Standards That a Man Knows How to Cook) so if you don't; you want to get that skill down first.

The freshly prepared salmon and avocado sauce will impress her. You can offer her chocolate again, unless she finished your chocolate reserves on the first date. That can happen.

But, if she hasn't succumbed by now, you might need to go to your "closer".

GREYHOUND PECAN SALADE

INGREDIENTS

Butter lettuce. . . . . 1 head

Grapefruit 1

Goat cheese . . . . 2 oz. (¼ cup)

Pecans. . . . . 2 oz. (¼ cup)

Avocado . . . . ½

Grapefruit Vinaigrette:

White wine vinegar . . . . 1 tablespoon

Olive oil . . . . 2 tablespoons

Juice from grapefruit . . . . 1 tablespoon

Step one

- Slice avocado
- Using a small, sharp knife, peel 1/2 of the grapefruit, removing all of the bitter white pith. Cut in between the membranes to release thin wedges, about 2 to 3 per section

Step two

Prepare grapefruit vinaigrette

- In a small cup mix 2 tablespoons of olive oil and 1 tablespoon each of white wine vinegar and grapefruit juice

Step three

- Place medium-sized whole leaves of butter lettuce on plate
- Shred center of lettuce into 1/4" strips and place on top of medium sized whole leaves

Step four

- Alternate slices of avocado with grapefruit wedges
- Sprinkle crumbled goat cheese and chopped pecans on top of salad
- Stir grapefruit vinaigrette well. Spread lightly over salad just before serving

Serves 2

Variation
Use other soft lettuces in place of butter lettuce Use crumbled blue cheese in place of goat cheese

SEAHAWK PASTA

INGREDIENTS

Avocado . . . . 1 large

Farfalle (bowtie shaped pasta) . . . . 6 oz.

Vegetable broth . . . . 1½ cups

Shallot 1

Salmon fillet . . . . ¾ – 1 lb.

Olive oil . . . . 2 tablespoons

Flour . . . . 1 tablespoon

Step one
- Bring 1 quart of water to boil with 1 tablespoon each of salt and olive oil

Step two
- Slice the salmon in approximately 1/2" squares
- Cut avocado into approximately 1/2" squares
- Mince (chop finely) the shallots

Step three
- Add pasta to boiling water for approximately 8 – 10 minutes. Do not overcook.

Step four
- Preheat 1 tablespoon of olive oil in pan
- Add minced shallot and cook over medium heat for approximately 2 minutes

Step five
- Add salmon to pan
- Lightly cook for 1 – 2 minutes
- While the salmon is cooking, sprinkle a teaspoon of flour over the salmon. Thickening flour preferred but regular all-purpose flour is fine.

Step six
- Add vegetable broth slowly to salmon and as contents begin to boil, reduce heat.
- Salt and pepper to taste
- Add a dash white or cayenne pepper should you want it spicy

Step seven
- Add cooked pasta, stir and then gently fold in avocado squares
- Serve on individual plate or pasta bowls

Hint
When pasta is done, drain through colander. Do not rinse with water.

Serves 2

It is best to time the cooking of the pasta with the completion of the sauce. There should be enough time to prepare the sauce while the pasta is cooking.

THE CLOSER

Some games count more than others. Better yet, some opponents are tougher than others. You can't rely on your ace to go the distance on such nights. When fruit and cheese or chocolate in the form of a bar is just not going to do it for her, you've got to be ready to go the bullpen and send your closer to the mound.

Your main course has put "Gettin' Some" up by one over "How 'Bout Lunch Next Week." In from the bullpen comes, "The Blue Collar Soufflé." It's the working man's version of the, "Need to order 30 minutes in advance," dessert at a swanky restaurant. Not here. You can't count on your personality to hold the lead that long. Fifteen minutes over cabernet, while clearing the plates and...Pow! The culinary equivalent of 3 'heaters' right down the middle.

Nice save!

INGREDIENTS

Butter (unsalted). . . . . 4 tablespoons

Eggs . . . . 2 large eggs

Sugar. . . . . 4 tablespoons

Bittersweet chocolate . . . . 4 oz.

Flour. . . . . 2 ½ tablespoons

Vanilla ice cream . . . . 2 scoops

Chocolate is to women what red meat is to guys. It's their nemesis, the kryptonite, and lifeblood they can't live without.

Step one

- Preheat oven to 400°. Put chocolate and butter in a double boiler over low heat and stir until chocolate is melted. (A mixing bowl on top of a sauce pan with a cup of water can be used in place of a double boiler.)

Step two

- In a small bowl or cup mix sugar and flour

Step three

- In a medium bowl whisk eggs, then whisk in flour and sugar

Step four

- Whisk in chocolate into egg mixture

Step five

- Scrape mixture into two 1 cup baking bowls (glass or ceramic called ramekins) and bake for approximately 15 minutes until edges are firm and center is still soft

Step six

- Add scoop of vanilla ice cream to center and serve immediately

Variation

Replace ice cream with whipped cream

Tip
Prepare steps one through four in advance and set aside.
This way, you simply have to place them in the oven after your final course.

Peer Review

She's probably boasted about you to her friends by now, and has invited them to join you both for a meal. No problem. That's what food's all about. You've established your willingness to cook and your skills at doing so. The only problem is, since you are the first guy to cook for her, she's most likely promoted you heavily to her friends. This means you've got to cook a notch above The Swing Date —though after that you're home free.

Your goal in the Peer Review is to make her look good in front of her friends —so be The Chef tonight. And don't be shy on the portions.

1st course

Lobster Spears

This exquisite appetizer should be served when the guests arrive, but certainly after they have been served a drink. Remember, it's not good to eat on an empty stomach. They're a tasty and classy starter and will be selling you even as guests are inspecting the photographs on your bookshelves and everything else.

2nd course

Prawns and Shreds

This salad allows for lots of variation in ingredients and is always a meal unto itself. The combination of so many complimentary ingredients, they most likely haven't tasted before, could cause suspicion you are a hired gun. Just accept the kudos gracefully since you know there are more on the way.

3rd course

Breakaway Shanks

This is a full-bodied dish that'll showcase your talent. You find it in restaurants and people will recognize it and appreciate it. There's a good chance the women will get full before they finish, but watch the guys clean up any remains.

Dessert course

Sensual Berries

Finish 'em off with papaya, raspberries and blueberries. It's light, tasty and good looking. Of course, never be afraid of complimenting that with some chocolate.

Since you are the first guy to cook for her, she's most likely promoted you heavily to her friends

Wow! You've done it. They're impressed (And if by chance, they're not impressed, you'll never win 'em over. Consider moving on).

After the Swing Date and Peer Review you can continue to romance her with different combinations of dishes for two- or three-course meals. I've added some additional recipes in the following pages to keep the flame burning.

Have fun.

LOBSTER SPEARS

INGREDIENTS

Raw lobster tails	8 oz. – 10 oz.
Parsley	6 sprigs
Belgian endive	2 stalks
Avocado	1
Chives (fresh)	12 strands
Mayonnaise	2 tablespoons

Step one

- Slice open lobster from underneath tail and remove meat
- Cut into 3/8" squares
- Slice avocado into thin 1/8" strips
- Mince (chop finely) chives

Step two

- Preheat 2 tablespoons of olive oil in pan
- Add lobster and cook over medium heat for approximately four minutes, stirring occasionally
- Let cool and place in small bowl
- Add mayonnaise and mix
- Salt and pepper to taste

Step three

- Remove twelve leaves from endive stalks
- Place 1 slice of avocado in each leaf
- Add a small portion of lobster mix on top of avocado
- Sprinkle minced chives on top of each spear
- Garnish with parsley and serve

Serves 4

PRAWNS & SHREDS

INGREDIENTS

Avocado . . . . .2 medium
Lemon. 1
Green onions . . . .¼ cup chopped
Bacon . . . . 2 strips
Lime 1
Cherry or baby tomatoes 20
Cilantro (fresh). . .¼ cup chopped
Iceberg lettuce . . . . .¾ head
Prawns (shrimp) . . . . .½ lb.
   raw/shelled/deveined

Cilantro Puree

Sour cream . . . . 6 tablespoons
Lime juice. . . . . 2 tablespoons
Cilantro leaves loosely packed. . . . . 1/3 cup

Step one

- Slice bacon into 1/8" strips and cook until crispy
- Remove and dry on paper towel

Step two

- Add prawns and lemon (cut in half and squeezed) to pot with 1 quart of water and bring to boil
- Shrimp should be done as soon as water is boiling
- Remove from stove and slightly cool with running water
- Cut shrimp into 1/2" pieces

Step three

Preparation of Cilantro Puree

- Combine ingredients and puree in a blender until smooth
- Salt and pepper to taste

Step four

- Cut tomatoes in half, chop lettuce, avocados and green onions in 1/2" squares
- Separate cilantro leaves from stems. Discard stems.
- Combine above ingredients in salad bowl
- Add dressing, toss and serve

Serves 4

BREAKAWAY SHANKS

INGREDIENTS

Veal shanks 4

Egg noodles . . . . .8 oz.

Fresh basil . . . . 4 - 6 sprigs

Onion 1

Chicken broth . . . . 2 cups

Tomatoes . . . . .4 medium

Flour . . . . ¼ cup

Olive oil . . . . 3 tablespoons

Step one

- Chop (dice) onions into 1/2" squares
- Flour veal shanks
- Preheat (1) tablespoon of olive oil in pan and pot
- Add onions to pan and cook over medium heat for approximately 4 minutes
- Add veal shanks to pot and brown on both sides

Option

Sauté onions and brown shanks simultaneously in same pot

Step two

- Add sautéed onions, tomatoes cut in 1/2" squares and chicken broth to veal shanks
- Bring to boil, lower heat and simmer until shanks are tender. (Approximately 2½ – 3 hours)

Step three

- About 15 minutes before serving bring two quarts of water to boil with 1 tablespoon each of salt and olive oil
- Add noodles and boiling water for 6 – 8 minutes

Step four

- Remove shanks from pot
- Transfer liquid to blender and blend
- Salt and pepper to taste
- Remove from blender and add to noodles

Step five

- Place noodles on plate
- Put veal shanks in center
- Slice basil leaves, top each plate and serve

Serves 4

51

SENSUAL BERRIES

INGREDIENTS

Papaya 1
Parsley . . . . .2 sprigs
Blueberries. . . . . .1 cup
Raspberries . . . . .1 cup
Lime 1

Step one

- Cut the papaya in half
- Scoop out the seeds with a spoon
- Squeeze 1/2 lime over the papaya to enhance the flavor

Note

Lime is important in this course. It brings out the flavor in the papaya.

Step two

- Fill papaya with blueberries and raspberries
- Slice remaining half of lime and add parsley for décor

Serves 2

Recipe can easily be doubled for guests.

1

This course can compliment a breakfast, lunch, dinner or be a dessert.

ROCKET & BELGIAN ENDIVE

INGREDIENTS

Arugula (Rocket) . . . . . .12 large leaves (6 oz.)

Pear. 1

Goat cheese . . . . .2 oz. (¼ cup)

Walnuts . . . . .2 oz. (¼ cup)

Belgium endive. . . . . .1 stalk

Orange Vinaigrette:

White wine vinegar . . . . 1 tablespoon

Olive oil . . . . 2 tablespoons

Orange . . . . .½

Step one

Prepare orange vinaigrette

- In small cup mix 2 tablespoons each of olive oil and orange juice and 1 tablespoon of white wine vinegar

Step two

- Spread arugula (rocket) on plate
- Slice pear and place on top in fan shape

Step three

- Slice Belgian endive into 1/4" strips
- Place on plate at base of fan

Step four

- Sprinkle crumbled goat cheese and chopped walnuts on top
- Mix orange vinaigrette well and spread lightly over salad just before serving

Serves 2

Variation

Replace goat cheese with blue cheese

Presentation is what adds to an otherwise simple salad.

SWAMP WATER SEA BASS

INGREDIENTS

Chilean sea bass . . . . ½ lb.

Watercress . . . . 4 sprigs

Curry powder . . . . .1 tablespoon

Butter lettuce. . . . . 2 leaves

Milk or half & half . . . . ¼ cup

Vegetable stock . . . . .1 cup

Step one

- Place lettuce, watercress, curry powder, vegetable stock and milk in blender
- Add mixture to small/medium pan

Step two

- Add sea bass filets
- Over medium/high heat poach fish until done (approximately 3 minutes)

Step three

- Transfer sea bass to medium sized flat soup bowl
- Add curry sauce just enough not to cover the sea bass
- Garnish with watercress sprig

Serves 2

Variation

Replace Chilean sea bass with halibut

FRESH INFIELD CUTS

INGREDIENTS

Papaya 1

Mesclun greens. . . . . .6 oz.

Grapefruit 1

Avocado. . . . . .1 ½

Almonds (sliced) . . . . 4 oz. (½ cup)

Lime 1-2

Grapefruit Vinaigrette:

Olive oil . . . . .2 tablespoons

White wine vinegar . . . . .1 tablespoon

Juice from grapefruit . . . . . . .1 tablespoon

Step one

- Preheat oven to 350°
- Place sliced almonds on cookie sheet and toast in oven for approximately 10 minutes
- Remove and save for serving

Step two

- Peel and slice avocado and papaya
- Using a small, sharp knife, peel ½ of the grapefruit, removing all of the bitter white pith. Cut in between the membranes to release thin wedges, about 2 to 3 per section

Step three

Prepare grapefruit vinaigrette

- In a small cup mix 2 tablespoons of olive oil and 1 tablespoon each of white vinegar and grapefruit juice

Step four

- Place mesclun greens on plate
- Alternate slices of avocado, grapefruit wedges and papaya
- Spread toasted almonds on top
- Stir vinaigrette well and spread lightly over salad just before serving

Serves 4

DERBY DAY SALMON

INGREDIENTS

Parsley or watercress leaves. . .1 tablespoon

Salmon steaks 2

Fresh grated horseradish root. . . . . . ¼ cup

Cucumber (peeled, seeded & sliced) . . . . ½

Breadcrumbs. . . . . ¼ cup

Sour cream . . . . ¼ cup

Mayonnaise . . . . .3 tablespoons

Step one
- Preheat oven to 450°
- Peel and grate horseradish root

Step two
- In a small bowl mix horseradish, bread crumbs and mayonnaise
- Salt and pepper to taste
- Mix well and store in the refrigerator until needed

Step three
- Spread horseradish mixture evenly over fish on top side
- Place salmon steaks on a lightly oiled baking sheet
- Bake filets for 10 – 12 minutes until fish is resilient when pressed at the thickest part

Step five
- Place cucumber, sour cream and parsley (or watercress) in a blender
- Salt and pepper to taste
- Transfer sauce to small pan and warm over low heat

Step six
- Place sauce on plate
- Place salmon on top, garnish and serve

Serves 2

Tip
Parsley or watercress leaves affect the color of the sauce. Less is better unless you prefer the sauce to appear bright green.

The Morning After

I've never awakened to a girl in my arms, looking at me with an infatuated gaze. How could she? I snore. There's no way she could get that close.

I used to flee in the morning.

"Uh … I gotta go to work," I'd stammer.

"Work? It's Sunday?" she'd ask.

A shrug of the shoulders and I was gone.

Poor move — based on inexperience and general panic. As you can imagine, my second-chance opportunities after such a move were slim.

I wish I had a chance to do it all over again. Then again, most of us do. I'm still uncomfortable, but now I flee to the comfort of the kitchen. I haven't left the building and she's surprised to wake to a pleasant breakfast. It's a good move.

(Author's note: If this book helps just one man on one Sunday morning, I will consider this project a success. Especially if that man is me!)

We've all been there. If you haven't made it this far, you need to seek better help than me. The rest of us know it's the trickiest of all situations to be in, but also the one most of us strive for — whether you met at a dinner party, friends introduced you, or you hooked up at a bar. The scenario is all the same: Someone was caught off-balance and that led to a chance romance. A rendezvous ended back at your place for a late evening of intimacy. Score!

Way to go! But the morning after is a whole new ballgame. The beauty, elegance and infatuation of last night are gone. You are now dealing with bloodshot eyes, morning breath and pillow hair. The elements of nature have turned against you at this moment. You need a momentum shift about now. A good breakfast can do the trick. It'll break the tension of your first morning together, or add adoration to the eyes of your long-time mate.

Note: Bagels, donuts and the like are a cute move — and you can get away with it, but so can the competition. Remember him: the guy with more hair, money, stamina, etc.? The idea is to break away from the competition.

Even if the meal isn't perfect, the pure chivalry of attempting to cook breakfast will be notable. Make a great breakfast and she'll boast to her friends when she gets together for the official review. That's right, the girls' club review — it does take place, so I am told. Your morning efforts in the kitchen might divert their conversation from any of your shortcomings to the meal you prepared the morning after, elevating you to Brad Pitt status. It's a win-win.

> **Note: Bagels, donuts and the like are a cute move — and you can get away with it, but so can the competition. Remember him: the guy with more hair, money, stamina, etc.?**

How to Win Celebrity Status

You want to prepare a breakfast she's never seen before. Visions will dance in her head: "This guy's worldly." "He's domestic." "He's caring." "He must be wonderful with kids." Her thoughts will redirect from the 2-minute marvel who snores like a wood chipper to "this guy's a keeper." (Not exactly what you were thinking, maybe, but they move faster than us on this stuff; upon introduction, they consider whether or not you would produce cute kids.)

Here are some examples. None of these breakfasts are common. I've taken the layering technique experienced at many fine restaurants and applied it to eggs. By stacking, you pick up the joint flavors with every bite. The end result is unique combinations that are both flavorful and picturesque. Many of the ingredients are interchangeable to give variety to the same dish. For the stud who has a new date every weekend, only one version is needed. For the rest of us — who have to impress the same audience every Sunday morning — we need to mix it up.

Sensual Eggs, consisting of layering fresh salmon, avocado and poached eggs, is a great dish to start with. It's impressive-looking and she most likely has never tasted the combinations. Fruit and berries will complete this ensemble. They, too, have an attractive presentation and are a delicious complement to the meal.

Eggs and the Other White Meat is an approach using fresh pork rather than salt-cured hams or bacon. Adding the natural flavors of the arugula and avocado make this dish a complete renovation of the old eggs and ham.

Harbor Hash and The Kingfish Benedict elevate once-blue-collar breakfasts to an epicurean level.

Similar to the Eggs and the Other White Meat theme, both Harbor Hash and The Kingfish Benedict elevate once-blue-collar breakfasts to an epicurean level. Seafood hash and a croissant with smoked salmon and dill hollandaise are mouth-watering.

The Stacked Deck is a no-brainer for a group breakfast. (Whoa ... slow down! I'm talking about inviting friends or family over for breakfast, not a swinger's sleepover.) The layering enables you to provide four to five different omelets at one time, and the flexibility makes it easy to accommodate preferred tastes without spoiling the dish for others. In California, we're blessed with avocados year round. I've provided some suggestions for alternative ingredients, but you can use whatever ingredients are indigenous to your area to create different versions. These breakfasts are a lot of fun.

Have a good morning.

SENSUAL EGGS

This meal has a sensual feel to it. The smooth textures of the pan seared salmon coupled with the avocado and poached egg is delectable. Salmon is considered the fish of love. I recommend this breakfast on the days where there are no plans. After this she might lead you back to the bedroom.

INGREDIENTS

Fresh salmon	2 thin slices
Parsley	2 sprigs
Tomato	½ small
Bacon	2 strips
Avocado	½
Eggs	2
Salt	1 tablespoon
Olive oil	½ teaspoon

Ingredients for single serving shown. The recipe can easily be doubled to serve two.

Step one

- Preheat a few drops of olive oil in pan
- Grill salmon and tomato for approximately 1 minute per side
- In other pan, grill bacon
- Fill medium pot to ½ to ¾ full of water
- Add 1 small tablespoon of salt and bring to boil while grilling salmon

Step two

- Place salmon and tomato on the plate as shown
- Slice avocado, place on top of salmon and arrange the avocado to use the shape of the slices to hold the eggs in place
- Cover to keep warm

Step three

- Crack eggs into boiling water
- Poach eggs to desired doneness 1½ – 2 minutes
- Remove eggs carefully with slotted spoon in order to drain all of the water

Step four

- Gently place poached eggs onto the avocado
- Place bacon on plate
- Garnish with parsley and serve
- Add tabasco for a little kick

Hint

If able to think a little quicker in the morning after, start the water boiling at the same time your are cooking the bacon.

Note

The salt will help the eggs stay together.
Some chefs add white vinegar to boiling water but it can alter the taste of the egg.
Salt works just fine.

HIS OMELET

INGREDIENTS

Eggs . . . . 3 large

Sausage. . . . . 1 medium or 2 small

American cheese. . . . . .2 slices or grated

Milk or cream . . . . 1 tablespoon

Hollandaise sauce. . . . . 1 tablespoon*

Fruit for garnish

*Use any canned hollandaise sauce available.

Ingredients for single serving shown. The recipe can easily be doubled to
serve two.

Step one
- Cut sausage into 3/8" pieces

Step two
- Heat small pan
- Add sausage and cook over medium heat until done (Approximately 3-5 minutes)
- Remove to paper towel

Step three
- Beat eggs in a bowl
- Mix hollandaise and milk into egg mixture thoroughly

Step four
- Preheat medium pan with 1 tablespoon of butter
- Pour egg mixture into pan
- Cook slowly over low heat to allow eggs to rise (or fluff)

Step five
- Add sausage and cheese in middle of eggs
- Gently fold over eggs
- Cover and cook for 30 seconds

Step six
- Serve with fruit garnish

Options
- Replace sausage with bacon or ham or use combination of two or three
- Add chopped bell peppers and/or onions in step two

Variation

Omit hollandaise and add additional tablespoon of milk or cream

Step Four Tip
Carefully lift edge of cooked eggs up and tilt pan to allow uncooked portion of eggs to pour under

KINGFISH BENEDICT

HOW TO MAKE KINGFISH BENEDICT

INGREDIENTS

Eggs . . . . 2 extra large

Croissant 1

Dill (fresh) . . . . 2 sprigs

Hollandaise sauce . . . . 2 tablespoons*

Smoked salmon . . . . .2 slices

*Use any canned hollandaise sauce available.

Ingredients for single serving shown.

The recipe can easily be doubled to serve two.

Step one

- Chop dill weed, mix with hollandaise sauce and warm in microwave or small sauce pan
- Slice croissant lengthwise in half and toast

Step two

- Melt small tablespoon of butter in small pan over low heat
- Crack two eggs and cook over easy

Step three

- Place half of the toasted croissant on a plate
- Add smoked salmon
- Add fried over easy eggs
- Top with hollandaise sauce and serve

Variation

Replace fried eggs with poached or scrambled eggs

EGGS AND THE OTHER WHITE MEAT

INGREDIENTS

Thin pork chop 1

American cheese . . . . 1 slice or grated

Arugula . . . . 1 oz.

Eggs 2

Avocado . . . . ½

Olive oil . . . . ½ teaspoon

Butter . . . . 1 tablespoon

Note — Arugula is the ingredient of choice but spinach can be used if arugula is unavailable.

Ingredients for single serving shown. The recipe can easily be doubled to serve two.

Step one

- With a wooden mallet, pound pork chop on bread board or cutting block, pounding both sides until the pork chop doubles in size.
- Beat eggs in a bowl
- Slice arugula into 1/4" strips
- Slice avocado (lengthwise)

Step two

- Heat two small non-stick pans simultaneously, place the pounded pork chop in one pan with a few drops of olive oil and melt a small tablespoon of butter in the other.
- Cook the pork chop approximately 1½ minutes on each side and scramble eggs in other pan

Step three

- Reduce heat on eggs and leave in pan to remain hot

Step four

- Place pork chop on plate
- Add arugula on top of pork chop
- Add slices of avocado on top of arugula

Step five

- Place scrambled eggs on top of the avocado
- Add slice of cheese or sprinkle grated cheese on top of eggs.
- Place plate in the microwave or under broiler for about 30 seconds to melt the cheese.
- Add the additional arugula for decoration and serve.

Variation

- Replace pork chop with thin sliced chicken breast
- Replace arugula with parsley

STACKED DECK

INGREDIENTS

Avocado . . . . ½ - 1
Creamed spinach . . . . ¼ cup
Cheese . . . . ¼ cup grated*
Sausage 2
Milk or cream . . . . 4 tablespoons
Eggs 8
Butter . . . . 4 tablespoons
*American, jack, mild cheddar or goat

Step one

- Brown sausage in a small pan for approximately 3 – 5 minutes
- Remove and chop into approximately 3/8" pieces
- Melt a small tablespoon of butter in each small non-stick pan (Minimum of two pans needed. Four will save time)
- Beat 2 eggs and 1 tablespoon of milk or cream (Repeat step 3 times)
- Add 2 beaten eggs to each pan and cook as a flat omelet over low heat approximately 3 – 4 minutes (do not scramble)
- Flip eggs as soon as they are firm enough to turn
- Low heat is important for eggs to rise and not turn brown

Step two

- As soon as eggs have been turned over, add creamed spinach to flat omelet in one pan.
- Repeat step in other pans for sausage, avocado and cheese

Step three

- Stack flat omelet from each pan on top of each other

Step four

- Slice in quarters and serve

Serves 4

Variation

You can substitute items in layers with alternatives such as bacon, ham, sautéed pepper/onions, various flavored sausages, chili and a variety of cheeses.

HARBOR HASH

This combination is as delectable as the Sensual Eggs but should be served on those mornings where you have plans for the rest of the day. Unlike sensual eggs, the hash doesn't leave you in the mood for love.

INGREDIENTS

Eggs 8

Onion . . . . 1 medium

Red potatoes . . . . 2 medium or 3 small

Hollandaise sauce . . . . 8 oz.*

Red bell pepper 1

Pasilla pepper 2

Juice from orange . . . . 2 tablespoons

Shrimp (shelled) . . . . ½ lb. (Preferably uncooked)

Dungeness crab meat . . . . ½ lb.

Olive oil . . . . 2 tablespoons

Butter . . . . 2 tablespoons

*Use any canned hollandaise sauce available

Step one

- Chop potatoes, peppers, onions and shrimp into 3/8" – 1/2" squares, shred crab into bite size pieces and mix in a bowl
- Heat equal amounts of olive oil and butter in a non-stick pan (approximately 1 teaspoon each to start).
- Cook mixture over medium heat until potatoes are done and hash has a brown crispy look
- Salt and pepper to taste
- Fill medium pot 1/2 – 3/4 full of water
- Add 1 small tablespoon of salt and bring to a boil while cooking hash

Hint

You may need to add more olive oil and butter along the way but less is better than more.

Step two

- Add 2 tablespoons of orange juice to hollandaise and stir
- Heat hollandaise in a separate saucepan or microwave

Step three

- Put hash on plate and have warm hollandaise sauce ready

Step four

- Crack eggs into boiling water
- Poach eggs to desired doneness 1½ – 2 minutes
- Remove eggs carefully with slotted spoon in order to drain all of the water

Step five

- Gently place poached eggs on top of hash
- Cover with warm hollandaise sauce
- Garnish and serve

Serves 4

Step One Note

The salt will help the eggs stay together.
Some chefs add white vinegar to boiling water but it can alter the taste of the egg. Salt works just fine.

Variation

Pasilla peppers vary in taste from mild to medium hot and are best suited to this dish. If the only peppers available are other mild green chilies or green bell peppers, use them, but add a very finely chopped jalapeno or serrano pepper to add a little spice to the hash!

FRUIT & CHEESE

This course can compliment a breakfast, lunch, or dinner or be a dessert.

INGREDIENTS

Mango 1

Parsley .2 sprigs

Bosque pear. 1

Strawberries . . . . 10 – 12

Camembert cheese. . . . . 3 – 4 slices

Step one

- Mangos have a flat seed that runs almost the length and width of the mango. The best way to cut is to take a knife at the long end and slide it through as close to the seed as possible. Turn the remaining part over and repeat the cut just above the seed to the other side. You will end up with two halves and the seed in the center with still some fruit on it

Step two

- Cut the mango lengthwise and across. It is important to slide the knife through the meat of the mango without cutting through the skin but stay as close as you can to the skin without penetrating the skin on the other side
- Using two hands, push upwards with thumbs on skin

Step three

- Slice the Bosque pear and strawberries approximately 1/4" thick
- Place slices of the Camembert on the Bosque pear and strawberry slices
- Garnish with parsley, remaining strawberries and serve

Variation

Other combinations of seasonal varieties of fruits more common or available can be an attractive and tasty addition, such as, peaches, apples, bananas and almost any berries.

BREAKFAST . . .
Her Place

You've got to be optimistic; I keep my refrigerator stocked for breakfast guests all of the time. I've had to eat more than my share of breakfasts and throw away some spoiled ingredients, but this is a small price to pay in order to be ready come game day.

But we never know when or where lightning is going to strike, and a properly stocked refrigerator at your place means nothing when you end up at her place. Waking up at her place is what we hope for, and if you've been paying attention, is also a great opportunity to impress her.

Great quarterbacks have shown us the skill to be able to audiblize at the line, work well inside a broken play and perform on the road. It's what separates the champions from the rest. Being able to cook something out of nothing has the same elevating results. Your ability to cook on your feet comes from practice (As a teenager, I would spend our summer mornings cooking eggs long before women ever entered the picture).

Detailed instructions are moot because we don't know exactly what ingredient we will be working with. This requires some trial and error on your part.

Have no fear. Realize that the ability to ad lib in the kitchen gets better with every experience, and it's impressive. I can give you the idea, but you have to run with it.

Your choices will most likely be limited to the typical items found in most kitchens, such as milk, eggs and fruit. Unbeknownst to her, there's a lot that you can do with the standard discoveries. Put a little personality into the dish, and she'll be amazed by the results.

Somethin' from nothin'...

There's a good chance, if you went out to dinner, that one of you brought back a doggie bag with some leftovers. Leftovers often provide unusual ingredients that go surprisingly well with the eggs that are most likely already there. The meat or fish can be re-grilled to go with fried eggs, and some vegetables from the night before work great in an omelet.

When leftovers aren't an option, typical ingredients can create pleasant surprises also. You're apt to find some fruit on the counter and a box of instant pancake mix in her cupboard. Adding a crushed banana and some nuts to the pancake mix will upgrade this old stand-by. Get a feel for combining various ingredients and give it a go.

We can all read recipes. Being able to begin to envision a meal out of items in a refrigerator comes with time. You think Elway was able to perform all of those two-minute drives on his first attempt? Of course not, he practiced.

Take my advice and begin to experiment. Practice on your own and you to will be prepared to produce when the game is on the line. You'll discover ways to create meals out of what appears to be nothing. This will prove to her that you are more than a recipe reader. You are a cook.

Some examples follow:

Dinners are big and many times our eyes are bigger than our stomachs. There are a few items that are often good to bring home. Meat, fish or poultry from the main course will always reheat. Vegetables, on the other hand, don't work as well the next day. Three exceptions are the baked potato and/or mashed potatoes and creamed spinach that are served at most steakhouses.

In addition to leftovers, you can plan on some standard ingredients from her refrigerator. Don't expect anything exotic, but most likely her preferred survival goods.

She is apt to have some basic fruit and vegetables along with sliced bread, eggs, cheese, sliced ham and some type of meat.

With a little ingenuity, these items can be used for both ingredients and decorative garnish. Aesthetics count for a good part of the meal, and properly highlight your efforts.

Follow steps from omelet recipe. Heat creamed spinach, add to omelet with slice of cheese and fold over eggs. Slice in half for presentation. Fan sliced fruit over lettuce leaves to enhance the display.

Bacon and eggs is a mainstay in American culture. It's simple, yet enjoyed by many. Include some fried potatoes and add garnish if available.

This is a good one to have in your playbook. Place ham and a slice of cheese between two slices of bread, dip into beaten egg (with a splash of milk or cream if available) and grill in a pan with melted butter. Similar to a Monte Cristo, but better because it is not deep fried. Tastes great with or without syrup for either sweet tooth or the grilled sandwich taste.

Something that you want to take home from dinner is the baked potato. Mashed potatoes work well, but the baked has extra flavor from the sour cream and chives. Remove potato from skin and add milk, butter or sour cream as if making mashed potatoes. Form the potato into palm size patties and grill. Grill the steak from the night before. Add scrambled eggs and toast with the potato patties to make a complete meal.

Your basic French Toast. There is a high probability she has these ingredients. Beat a couple of eggs in a bowl (add 1 – 2 tbs of milk or cream, if available), dip the bread slices into the egg mixture and grill in a pan until brown. Sprinkle with cinnamon, powdered sugar or nutmeg, if discovered. Serve with sliced fruit and you arc a hero.

People rarely use chicken or fish for breakfast, but it will surprise you. Take a leftover chicken breast or salmon from the night before, dice along with a little onion. Melt a tablespoon of butter in a medium pan until hot, add diced onion, chicken or salmon and cook for approximately 2 minutes. Turn heat to low. Beat 2-4 eggs adding 1 tablespoon of milk per 2 eggs, if available. Pour in pan over chicken or fish and scramble. Good chance she has a tomato. Cut it in half and grill it in a pan.   Grilled tomatoes are a common side dish to eggs in England and Australia and make a good addition.

Note — With raw chicken, make sure chicken is cooked before adding egg mixture.

Pancakes are often made thick and doughy. You can improve. In a bowl, thin any mix with some milk. The pancake will come out thin and resemble more of a crepe. To really enhance these cakes, and move you up the ladder, mash a ripe banana into the mix and add some chopped nuts. The flavor will be in the pancake itself and can be enjoyed with or without the syrup if desired. Grill in non-stick pan with oil over medium/high heat. Test one. They must be golden brown since looks are 70% of this dish.

Warning — if you can't find these ingredients and all she has is celery and carrot sticks, the corner café will have to come into your playbook.

The Weekend Pass

Tailgating is where it's at! You rarely get lucky in a stadium parking lot with the guys, but there's more to life than chasing women — namely, sports.

Let's take a break from courtship for a moment. We could use a break from women by now, and I'm sure they feel the same.

Most relationships need a break, also. I'm one to dive into a new date and spend lots of time together. Then, after a few weeks, it's back to planning weekends with the guys. You might know what I'm talking about. Once you've landed a date, the pendulum swings. Out goes the all-day-in-bed Saturdays and walks on the beach, and back comes the tailgate party, hunting and fishing trips, golf rounds, and road trips.

All right … all right … I've never taken a romantic walk on the beach, but the idea excites most women.

Tailgating

Unless you were fortunate enough to be in the stands for Franco Harris' immaculate reception, Kirk Gibson's walk-off home run off Dennis Eckersley in the '88 World Series, or some of the other miracles in sports, the games and scores tend to blend together over time. You rarely remember the mid-season results of the game, but the parking lot grill stays with you for years.

I grew up going to the Rose Bowl in Pasadena, California, with my family and a large group of friends. From parade to pre-game, kickoff, and the game itself, this event is an all-day affair. It's also where I gained my admiration and passion for the tailgate party. I was 7.

The motor coaches from the Midwest roll into town a week in advance in hopes of landing premiere parking spaces. Come game day, you can smell the grills throughout the Arroyo. There are limited routes into the canyon where the stadium sits and traffic can be a bear. Our group always made it a point to get there early and stay late. The majority of the day was spent horsing around in the parking lot. We'd have a huge pre-game celebration, and no matter how tight the game was, Big Ed would make his way to the parking lot midway through the third quarter to prep his third-generation Navy Bean soup or infamous chili for the post-game treat while the rest of the fans battled the traffic out of the canyon.

The country is filled with tailgates that begin hours before kickoff, cooking up mountains of grub, to complete display of excess. That's my kind of party.

The college football tradition remains the biggest turn-on in sports for me. There's no other sport more dedicated to celebrating food than college football. The country is filled with tailgates that begin hours before kickoff, cooking up mountains of grub, to complete display of excess. That's my kind of party.

Sporting weekends with friends

Cooking up a big meal is nothing new to many of you. I recall father-and-son hunting trips when I was young. Every father had a dish that he was known for. I'd offer to help prepare the food. I considered it fun and many times cooks would be excluded from bird-cleaning duty, a definite plus. "TV" Bill would always cook German potatoes and "Moosebelly" would slave over ricotta pancakes. While the meals were good, they became boring over the years. My Old Man once again provided the spark. He came with something new every time.

Having the talent to produce more than one dish for your buddies pays dividends. I learned from the Old Man's efforts; the guys were always looking forward to what he was going to cook. You can do the same for your group of friends.

I've also been on those trips where someone was assigned to go to the warehouse grocer to stock up on hot dogs and chips for survival. I was fresh out of high school at the time, and the pallet of beer took precedence over any food for the precious space in the truck bed. They were good times, but now that we have grown out of the spring-break trips, our weekends consist of a little more gourmet eating, along with the drinking. You still need to send someone for the beer and wine, but leave the hot dogs and chips for the kids. Everyone will appreciate the upgrade.

> **"It is not whether you win or lose, but how you play the game." You got that right, coach!**

In addition to hunting, we sailed. The annual event that I'm most familiar with is the Newport Beach, California to Ensenada, Mexico yacht race held every April. For years I've sailed with the same crew, which has included my father from time to time. Are we invited back because we are good sailors? No. A proven chef in the galley trumps even the best tactician for the limited crew openings on this race.

While the rest of the fleet is removing excess fuel and equipment to lighten the weight of the boat for the race, our crew is scurrying down the dock with cartloads of Cabernet and provisions to get us through the next couple of days at sea. That same competition supplies their crew with tuna sandwiches, some beer and a bag of chips. We post the race menu complete with wine pairings onto the bulkhead in order to motivate our troops. Hungry soldiers can't fight is the motto. The boat has become the envy of the fleet because eating and drinking is as important as trying to win.

In my Little League days, the coaches were always harping, "It is not whether you win or lose, but how you play the game." You got that right, coach!

Eat, drink, hunt, sail, football … allow me to take a moment to compliment my parents on a well-rounded upbringing.

To the grill...

I have cherry-picked a few favorites that we have cooked over the years. They are both flavorful and can be cooked in large quantities with relative ease. A brief scan of these recipes will give you the idea. This is the carnivores' section.

We're meat-eaters. "Never trust a man who doesn't eat meat," I've been told. (I told you the Old Man was full of one-liners.) He's never given me any reasoning behind the statement, but I haven't questioned the logic. Besides, in my circle of friends, I've yet to meet a man who doesn't eat meat. I start with barbecue selections because it is the most common heat source at a tailgate party, and I haven't forgotten who my audience is; I know your affinity for the 'que.

Eat, drink, hunt, sail, football ... allow me to take a moment to compliment my parents on a well-rounded upbringing.

Every man believes he's a grill expert. Handling the grill duties validates masculinity. So be it.

Pigskin Spedinis are simple sirloin skewers grilled with horseradish and Parmesan cheese. The preparation is time-consuming, so get your friends to help; they'll enjoy participating in the process. Spedinis work great at any barbecue party.

Hot dogs, ribs and chicken wings are mainstays in the testosterone diet. I've upgraded the hot dog using a Midwestern tailgate favorite, the bratwurst. Simmer the sausages in beer and onions to set up the flavor. Serve in a fresh roll with mustard, pickles and onions from the broth. Your crew won't be able to stop eating these.

My wings can be prepared as hot as you want and are free from the heavy sauce or batter found at most sports bars. I serve them with a cucumber dipping sauce to add a cool complement to the hot wing. It's a refreshing change from the ranch or blue cheese dressing usually offered.

Baby back ribs grilled slowly end up tender and juicy and are served with a natural sauce created from a blend of vegetables. Your carnivorous friends will enjoy the break from the common bottled sauces that usually overpower the meat.

If you're over-nighting at a place with a kitchen or can do the preparation in advance, I recommend Mustang Ranch Quail and/or 4th and Goal Short Ribs. The Mustang Ranch Quail is a gourmet version of fried chicken. These are small fowl, and all of the meat is close to the bone to provide juicy flavor in every bite. Leave the utensils in the drawer; these birds require hands and teeth, and allow the guys the joy of cleaning the bone.

I consider 4th and Goal Short Ribs the signature dish of the book. As with many of my recipes, the flavor of the sauce comes from the ribs themselves. You can see by the preparation that this dish requires some extra equipment if you want to cook it at the game (i.e., a propane burner to heat the pot). If you're not that equipped, I suggest you cook them the night before. Place the pot in the refrigerator overnight. In the morning, remove the grease layer that has settled on top and re-heat before the game. The extra time in the pot enables the flavors to set up. Come game time these will melt in your mouth.

When cooking this dish the night before, be sure to add a couple of extra ribs. No one I know has the self-control to place the pot in the fridge without sampling a little for themselves.

Most men I have met are content with a big pile of meat, but in an attempt to provide a little fiber for colon relief, I've included the following salads that are hearty and add a little roughage to the carnivores' section.

By now, I hope you understand the flexibility of the dishes. The salads, appetizers from the potluck section, and/or any of the date dinners can be prepared for larger groups or parties. Depending on the event, use your judgment and newly acquired abilities to assemble the necessary complements to the selections that follow.

One final note: If the word is out on your cooking, plan on some party-crashers and cook extra. People eat more when they are out of town. If it is good, they're going to want seconds and you will want to satisfy.

See you in the parking lot.

PIGSKIN SPEDINIS

INGREDIENTS

Top sirloin steak . . . . 2 pounds

Fresh grated Parmesan cheese . . 4 oz. (½ cup)

Horseradish . . . . 4 oz. (½ cup)

Wooden skewers 24

Step one

• Slice top sirloin lengthwise in very thin strips (approximately 1/8" thick)

Step two

• Rub horseradish on both sides of strips

• Sprinkle parmesan cheese on both sides

• Slide skewer through strips so that meat will hold while grilling

Step three

• Grill over medium heat (1 – 2 minutes on each side)

Step four

• Serve

Depending on your friends, people can eat 4 to 40 of these morsels.

99

TAILGATE BRATWURST

INGREDIENTS

Bratwurst	12
Beer	2–3
Onions	2 medium
Dijon mustard	1 jar
Pickles	1 jar
Rolls	12

Step one

- Slice onions in 3/8" thick
- Place onions, bratwurst and beer in large pot
- Refrigerate until ready to cook

Overnight is great, but 30 minutes before kickoff will work.

Step two

- Remove brats and barbeque or grill slowly on low to medium heat until brown turning frequently. Be careful not to burn
- Return browned brats to pot with beer and onions
- Bring to a boil then lower heat and simmer for 1 hour

Step three

- Remove brats to a platter and place onions in a bowl
- Toast buns and serve

Preferred compliments

Beer, potato salad, beer, Dijon mustard and beer.

Serves 6 – 12

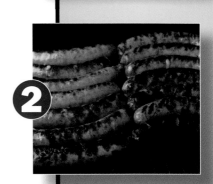

NAKED WINGS

INGREDIENTS

Chicken wings 24

Green bell pepper . . . . ½

Cayenne pepper . . . . .to taste

Chives. . . . . 1 bunch

Sour cream . . . . 4 oz. (½ cup)

Cucumber. .½

Butter . . . . ½ pound

Step one

- Fold tip of wing behind drumette
- Sprinkle with cayenne pepper
- Barbeque over medium heat or in oven at 500° for approximately 25 minutes
- Coat with melted butter frequently, while cooking

Step two

- Cut cucumber and bell pepper in 1/2" squares
- In blender add cucumber, bell pepper, sour cream
- Blend and salt to taste
- Mince chives and add to sauce

Step three

- Serve hot with cucumber cooling sauce

Variation

Replace chives with parsley

Serves 2 – 12 depending on their appetites

1

For extra hot wings, be more generous with the cayenne but have mercy

DEFENSELESS RIBS

INGREDIENTS

Pork ribs	1 rack
Baby back ribs	1 rack
Shallots	1
Limes	2
Tomatoes	4 medium
Chicken broth	½ cup
Worcestershire sauce	1 – 2 tablespoons
Molasses	2 tablespoons
Flour	½ teaspoon

Step one

- Grill ribs slowly on a low heat barbeque or oven at 275° for two hours (tenderness is achieved by lower temperatures and slower cooking. For example 225° at four hours)
- Salt and pepper ribs during grilling

Step two

- While ribs are grilling:
- Mince shallot
- Cut tomatoes into 3/8" squares
- Heat 1 tablespoon of olive oil in pan
- Add shallots and cook for 2 minutes
- Add tomatoes and cook for 4 minutes
- Add 1/2 teaspoon thickening flour and stir
- Add chicken broth to desired thickness
- Add juice from limes (approximately 2 tablespoons), molasses and Worcestershire sauce and mix thoroughly

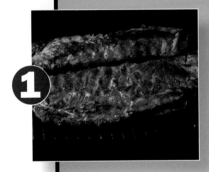

Step three

- Serve ribs on platter with sauce for dipping

Variation

Replace 2 tablespoons of molasses with 4 tablespoons of brown sugar

FOURTH & GOAL SHORT RIBS

INGREDIENTS

Flour . . . . ½ cup

Chicken broth . . . . 3 cups

Onion . . . . 1 ½

Short ribs . . . . 10 lbs.

Olive oil . . . . 2 – 3 tablespoons

Note
Great dish to be prepared in advance and can be reheated on location.

Step one

- Flour, salt and pepper short ribs on all sides

Step two:

- Chop onion in approximately 1/2" squares
- Preheat 1 tablespoon of olive oil in large pan
- Add onions and cook over medium heat for approximately 5 minutes and remove from heat

Step three

- Preheat 1 tablespoon of olive oil in a seperate pan
- Brown short ribs on all sides

Step four

- Once all of the short ribs have been browned, return them to the pot
- Add sautéed onions and chicken broth
- Cover and bring to boil, reduce heat and simmer for approximately 2½ hours or until short ribs are tender
- Stir and move the ribs around periodically in order for them to cook evenly

Step five

- Serve the ribs on a platter or on individual plates
- The remaining mixture in the pot will be perfect gravy
- Salt and pepper to taste

Tip

You can also put the gravy in a blender for a smooth texture.

Step Three Hint
Remove the onions from the pan and set aside so that you can brown the additional short ribs at the same time.

MUSTANG RANCH QUAIL

INGREDIENTS

Quail 12
Flour . . . . 1 cup
Olive oil . . . . 1 cup
Butter . . . . 1 cup

Step one

- Cut through quail breast and flatten
- Flour on both sides

Step two

- Preheat large pan and add equal parts of olive oil and butter (start with 1 tablespoon each)
- Using medium heat brown on both sides until done (approximately 5 minutes per side)
- Salt and pepper while cooking
- Continue process until all quail are cooked adding equal parts of oil and butter to pan each time

Step three

- Arrange on platter and serve

Serves 2 – 10 depending on your friends

SHELLFISH CLIPPINGS

INGREDIENTS

Iceberg lettuce	1 head
Ketchup	2 tablespoons
Eggs	6
Mayonnaise	4 tablespoon
Prawns (raw & deshelled)	1/3 lb.
Crabmeat (cooked)	1/3 lb.
Bay scallops (raw)	1/3 lb.
Parsley	8 sprigs
Lemon	1
Olive oil	1 tablespoon

Step one

- Place eggs in pot of cold water
- Bring water to boil uncovered. Then cover with lid, turn off heat and let eggs stand for ten minutes
- Place the pot with the eggs under faucet with cold running water until eggs are cool (approximately 2 minutes)

Step two

- Cut prawns into 1/2" squares
- Preheat tablespoon of olive oil in pan
- Add prawns and scallops over high heat
- Heat for approximately 4 minutes
- Add crab and cook for 4 more minutes, stirring occasionally
- Drain off remaining liquid from scallops and discard

Step three

- Chop lettuce, eggs and parsley in approximately 1/2" squares and place in salad bowl
- Add scallops, prawns and crab

Step four

- In a small bowl mix mayonnaise and ketchup
- Add to salad bowl, toss and serve

Serves 4

NAPA RUFFAGE

INGREDIENTS

Duck legs	4
Bean sprouts	4 oz.
Won ton wrappers	10
Red bell pepper	½
Green bell pepper	½
Napa cabbage	1 head
Olive oil	4 tablespoons
Cayenne pepper	dash

Raspberry Vinaigrette:

Raspberries	½ cup
Olive oil	4 tablespoons
White wine vinegar	2 tablespoons

Step one

- Preheat oven and roast duck legs at 350° for 1 hour
- Remove skin and cut duck, red and green peppers into 1/4" by 1" strips
- Slice cabbage into1/4" slices
- Slice won ton wrappers into 3/8" strips

Step two

- Preheat 4 tablespoons of olive oil in pan
- Cook separated strips over high heat for about 30 seconds on each side, use tongs to turn
- Remove from pan when brown and place on paper towel
- Sprinkle lightly with cayenne and save these "peppered crunchies" for later

Step three

Prepare raspberry vinaigrette puree

- Mash raspberries with a fork
- In a small cup, add 4 tablespoons of olive oil, 2 tablespoons of white wine vinegar and 2 tablespoons mashed raspberries

Step four

- Combine cabbage, sprouts, peppers, duck in salad bowl
- Just before serving add raspberry vinaigrette puree and peppered crunchies, toss and serve

Serves 4

SPRING TRAINING SALAD

Great side dish for any of the previous meat dishes in this section.

INGREDIENTS

Celery	3 – 4 stalks
Potatoes	12 medium brown
Onion	1
Eggs	8 – 10
Mayonnaise	8 oz. (1 cup)
Mustard	2 oz. (¼ cup)
Dill pickles	8 oz. (1 cup – sliced or whole)
Parsley	1 bunch

Step one

- Peel potatoes and cut in quarters
- Place cut potatoes in large pot, cover with water and boil until done (when fork penetrates the potato easily) approximately 30 minutes

Step two

- Place eggs in a pot of cold water
- Bring to a boil uncovered. Then cover with lid, turn off heat and let eggs stand for ten minutes
- Place the pot with the eggs under the faucet with cold running water until eggs are cool (approximately 2 minutes)

Step three

- Chop celery, onions, pickles and parsley into 1/8" squares
- Cut cooked potatoes and hard boiled eggs in 1/2" squares

Step four

- In large bowl combine potatoes, eggs and equal amounts of onions, celery, pickles and parsley
- Add salt and pepper while tossing so that salt and pepper is evenly distributed

Step five

- Mix mayonnaise and Dijon mustard in separate bowl
- Add to salad and toss until evenly spread
- Salt and pepper to taste if needed

Step six

- Cover with plastic wrap and refrigerate before serving

Her Bunco Night Potluck

We're great at using activities to get out of the house, but there's a lesson to be learned from women.

For decades, we've remained true to the traditional poker night gathering, which consists of lots of beer, some munchies, and a few smokes. The party favors haven't changed.

Women have embraced the bunco night. Bunco's the women's answer to poker. It's a dice game, it's a women's club, and it's her business.

Bunco has replaced bridge as the new social event. It's a game of chance and fun without the stress and intensity of a bridge match, so it allows for plentiful conversation — the real reason most of us want to get together in the first place. The game's just a clever disguise to get together (sounds similar to many of the golf tournaments I've played in).

Bunco's the women's answer to poker. It's a dice game, it's a women's club, and it's her business.

They spearheaded the potluck concept to accompany their games. The idea of splitting the workload among the invited guests is ingenious — what a sharp move by them.

Potluck has become the standard for her bunco night. We should be ashamed. While they're feasting on a variety of dishes during their competition, we continue to limit ourselves to beer and smokes. I've yet to see someone challenge the tradition. Imagine if a guy showed up to poker night with a plate of foie gras. He'd never be invited back,

Come game time, when her friends are comparing their mates for — well, just about everything — your woman'll quietly smile.

no matter how bad a player. Poker isn't ready for such culinary advances.

I've provided some recipes for you to cook for her night out. I know what you're thinking: "Recipes for her bunco night? I thought this book was for me." Hang on. The recipes are good, and the benefits to the cook are better.

At any good bunco gathering, the competition plays out more on the snack table than the dice game. These dishes will provide your lady with an edge over her friends. Yes, you figured it out, the ulterior motive — the reward for your efforts.

Having said that, whether it's a bunco night or a Little League team party, if you've been asked to bring something to the event and someone's beaten you to "ice duty," be assured that I've aligned a handful of simple, elegant preparations that are bound to impress. Even if her group is tired of hearing about her kid's Little League quests — which they are — the hors d'oeuvres will keep her in next month's game. Remember, the cook is always invited back.

Most of these recipes are for finger foods, which is sensible at a potluck. I've added a little elegance to the deviled egg, and used endive spears again because they're a perfect edible basket; whether lobster, chicken, or shrimp, the boat-shaped Belgian endive is ideal.

The success of the Longhorn Canapes lies in the cut of meat. Buy a good filet and you're rounding third base before turning on the stove … ingredients, ingredients, ingredients.

In addition to the finger foods, I've included a tasty cold soup. When transporting dishes, it's much easier to keep items cold than hot, so cold soups are ideal for a potluck.

Come game time, when her friends are comparing their mates for — well, just about everything — your woman'll quietly smile. The delicacies will begin to be consumed, and in a moment or two someone'll acknowledge the wonderful appetizer.

"Where did you learn to make this?" they'll ask.

Again, just a smile, knowing she has the upper hand.

"Really, where did you learn to do this?" will follow.

"I didn't have time, so my husband/boyfriend made it for me."

Conversation will stop. The dice will drop to the floor. There'll be silence never before experienced in the gossip-laden world of bunco.

As the initial shock wanes and consciousness returns to their faces, the color of their cheeks will begin to turn green as the envy fills the room. The other women won't be able to contain themselves. The thoughts of domestic equality will fill their heads: "He wears the apron, buys the groceries, vacuums, and the toilet seat is never left up."

Game, set, and match! She's won before the first die rolls out of the cup. Her friends' endorsements will elevate your new talents and validate her choice in a man. She'll be gleaming with pride.

My advice to you: Be ready when she gets home.

Conversation will stop. The dice will drop to the floor. There'll be silence never before experienced in the gossip-laden world of bunco.

Author's note: If, at this point, you have not capitalized on any lovin' from your cooking efforts, there is a high probability she's got someone on the side.

ENDIVE SPEARS

INGREDIENTS

Belgium endive . . . . 2 stalks

Cilantro . . . . 4 sprigs

Limes 3

Goat cheese . . . . 2 – 3 oz. (¼ – ½ cup)

Chicken breast . . . . 1 large breast

or ½ lb. ground chicken

Walnuts . . . . 1/4 cup

Shallots 1

Chicken broth . . . . ½ cup

Step one

- Cut the limes in half and squeeze the juice into a cup
- Mince shallots and the chicken breast (If possible purchase ground chicken from the butcher and save this step.)
- Chop walnuts

Step two

- Preheat 1 tablespoon of olive oil in pan
- Add minced shallot and chicken and cook over medium heat for approximately 10 minutes
- Add equal parts of lime juice and chicken stock (approx. 3 tablespoons)
- Salt to taste
- Sauté for a bit longer until chicken has turned white (approx. 3 minutes). Remove from heat. Leave ingredients in pan to cool.

Step three

- Spread endive leaves in a circular pattern around the plate
- Add approximately 2 tablespoons of the chicken to each leaf
- Add crumbled goat cheese on top of each leaf
- Sprinkle with chopped walnuts
- Add 2 – 3 cilantro leaves to each spear
- Garnish with additional cilantro in the center

Serves 4

Tip
Put goat cheese in freezer 5-10 minutes before crumbling

LONGHORN CANAPES

INGREDIENTS

Filet mignon	1 lb.
Chives	12 strands
Sourdough baguette	1
Sour cream	½ cup
Horseradish	¼ cup

Step one

- Preheat oven to 350°
- Slice filet and baguette (removing crust is optional) in 1/4" slices
- In a small bowl add the horseradish to the sour cream, mix together (approximately 3 – 4 tablespoons sour cream to 1 tablespoon horseradish)

Step two

- Toast baguette slices in oven (approximately 10 minutes)
- Heat a few drops of oil in pan
- Turn to high heat
- Brown filet slices on each side (approximately 30 seconds on each side)

Step three

- Spread the horseradish sauce on the bread
- Add a slice of the filet mignon, top with chopped chives and serve

Variation

Tender cuts of lamb loin can also be used

CUCUMBER SOUP

INGREDIENTS

Onion	¼ of 1 medium
Cucumbers (peeled)	2
Cilantro	10 sprigs
Sour Cream	¼ cup
Milk	¼ cup
Chicken broth	¼ cup

Step one

- Peel cucumber and cut into quarters
- Remove cilantro leaves from stems
- Cut onion into quarters

Step two

- Place cucumber, cilantro and onion in blender
- Add milk, sour cream, chicken broth and salt
- Blend for 5 –10 seconds

Step three

- Refrigerate
- Serve cold
- Garnish with cilantro leaves

Serves 4 – 6

HARDBALL EGGS

INGREDIENTS

Parsley	4 sprigs
Eggs	10
Mayonnaise	2 tablespoons
Parmesan cheese	1 tablespoon
Dijon mustard	1 teaspoons
Nutmeg	1 teaspoon

Step one

- Place eggs in a pot of cold water
- Bring to a boil uncovered. Then cover with lid, turn off heat and let eggs stand for ten minutes
- Place the pot with the eggs under the faucet with cold running water until eggs are cool (approximately 2 minutes)

Step two

- Next gently crack the eggs on the side of the pan and peel the shell off the eggs and cut peeled eggs in half lengthwise

Step three

- Remove yolk from egg by holding the egg that has been cut in half with two hands, gently press on the white side with your thumb and the yolk should fall out
- Place yolks in a bowl and mash with a fork
- Add Dijon mustard, mayonnaise, salt and pepper to taste. The approximate amounts for 10 egg yolks are about one teaspoon of Dijon mustard and two tablespoons of mayonnaise
- Once mixed, place the mixture back in the egg whites using a spoon

Step four

- On 1/3 of eggs add fresh grated parmesan cheese and place under broiler to brown cheese (2 – 3 minutes)
- Mince parsley (1 tablespoon)
- On the remaining eggs sprinkle half with nutmeg and half with minced parsley
- Arrange on plate and serve

Serves 6 – 10

CHICK CHEESES

The cheese plate can be used for breakfast, brunch, hors d'oeuvres or after dinner. A perfect follow up for after dinner especially in lieu of dessert for those who prefer a high protein and low carb lifestyle.

INGREDIENTS

Camembert cheese	8 oz. (1 cup)
(if you can not find Camembert, Brie would be a good choice)	
Goat cheese	8 oz. (1 cup)
Sourdough baguette	1
Saint Andre cheese	8 oz. (1 cup)
Blue cheese	8 oz. (1 cup)
Bosque pear	1
Jarlsberg cheese	8 oz. (1 cup)
Assorted berries	¼ cup of each
Parsley	2 sprigs

Note

Other cheeses can be substituted to the preparer's or to the audience's taste. This five-cheese combination is tasty with different flavors. Bosque is a pear of choice but others will suffice.

Step one

- Slice pear in 1/4" slices
- Add slices of the Camembert on top of pear slices
- Slice and arrange the remainder of bread and cheeses decoratively as shown
- Add berries, parsley and serve

Serves 8 – 10

LEMON PEPPER PRAWNS

INGREDIENTS

Medium raw shrimp .... 2lbs. (peeled/deveined)

Flour..2 tablespoons

Vegetable broth............................. 8 tablespoons (½ cup)

Half and half ....6 tablespoons

Cilantro (fresh leaves) .... ½ cup

Onion...½ Medium

Green bell pepper...½

Parsley (fresh leaves) .... ½ cup

Jalapenos (fresh).. 2

Tomatoes .... 2 Medium

Lemon 1

Olive oil ....3 tablespoons

Step One

Prepare salsa

- Dice equal parts tomatoes, bell pepper, onion in 1/4" squares
- Remove seeds from jalapeno and mince
- Chop parsley and cilantro
- Mix ingredients in bowl
- Add salt to taste
- Let stand

Step two

- Preheat 3 tablespoons of olive oil in large pan
- Add shrimp and fry over high heat. Cook for 1 – 2 minutes per side
- When almost done, sprinkle flour in pan with shrimp. Stir

Step three

- Reduce heat. Add juice from lemon (approximately 4 tablespoons), half and half and broth to pan. Stir
- Add 3 heaping tablespoons of salsa. Stir

Step four

- Place contents on platter and serve

Serves 6 – 8

Jalapenos spice can vary dramatically. Add with caution depending on your audience.

GAME NIGHT WINGLETS

HOW TO MAKE GAME NIGHT WINGLETS

INGREDIENTS

Chicken drumettes....................24

Lemon 1

Sour cream ....4 tablespoons

Lime.............................1

Dijon mustard.............1 tablespoon

Mayonnaise...............1 tablespoon

Step one
- Cut skin and force meat to thickest end of drumette
- Using two hands, force meat over end of bone leaving a ball of meat at the end

Step two
- Lightly flour winglets

Step three
- Preheat 3 tablespoons of olive oil in a large pan
- Brown winglets on all sides

Step four
- Transfer winglets to roasting pan
- Preheat oven to 375° and cook for 45 minutes

Step five
Prepare Dipping Sauce
- Grate 1 tablespoon each of lemon and lime peel
- In a small bowl squeeze 1 tablespoon each of lemon and lime juice from left over lemon and lime
- Add sour cream, mayonnaise, Dijon mustard, lemon and lime peels, a dash of pepper and mix

Step six
- Place dipping sauce in small bowl in center of platter
- Arrange winglets and serve

Serves 4 – 8

The Holidays

My family rifles through gossip faster than talk radio, and when they run dry of fresh material after approximately 13 minutes, the "Are you going to get married?" question takes center court.

Every man within the house is a target.

It's a question that piques most women's interest, and one that I prefer to avoid. It's a no-win situation. A "no" answer leaves them asking why, and a "yes" answer sets up the remainder of the day discussing the endless wedding details. I want to eat and watch football. Unfortunately, the question surfaces every time I bring a date.

The married guys are hardly exempt. "When are you going to have children?" is quick to follow the marriage question. Baby names, gender preferences, bedroom renovations — the details are never-ending. There's no acceptable objection; they want to see babies crawling around the furniture. If you're cornered, the pressure to succumb to their reproductive needs mounts.

(And don't think you're exempt if you aren't being asked either of these questions. If no one is confronting you, "Do you think he's gay?" is being asked in the other room.)

Having never been married and with no children of my own, I've found that the kitchen is the best place to hide. Even if I'm not the cook, I attempt to make myself useful in the kitchen. The helping hand is always well received in my family and appears to grant some immunity from the nuptials inquiry. The kitchen is a safe harbor.

As far as the food goes, we've always been aggressive about trying new dishes and the holidays are no exception.

We alternated households on the holidays between the various cousins and in-laws, but our house was always chosen for extra holidays. It was designed for entertaining, with a kitchen remodeled around a six-burner restaurant stove geared to handle big dinners. My Old Man has always taken entertaining seriously, and he prided himself on quality presentations for us to enjoy. Ingredients were bought at specialty grocers, and his preparation was thought out well in advance.

We got bored with the traditional fare when I was still very young. There have been years away from family when I've visited the households of various friends, relatives, and girlfriends for the holiday dinner. Some were non-cooking households that relied heavy on the spiral-cut ham and cranberry sauce from a can. I realized that my family is definitely not the norm, and am thankful for it.

Most people look forward to the traditional dinner and have never considered an alternative to stuffed turkey, ham and mashed potatoes. They associate the meal with this time of year and feel it is their patriotic duty to serve such fare. Through my years, I've observed that for many households, this is the only time of the year that they actually do cook.

What a great opportunity. People — including your family or, better yet, her family — love to be treated to dinner. A special dinner will be even more well-received. And you can figure that if her family is pleased with you, she will be pleased. You could get lucky again.

But beware! Families are critical and, as I've seen, resistant to change. For most, Mom is a tough act to follow. Of course, Mom will probably be the most approving of the effort. Go figure.

To try to satisfy as many as possible, I've included two complete holiday menus for your guests to enjoy. You determine which one will be best received. Everyone could use a reprieve from the predictable turkey, spiral-cut ham, mashed potatoes, candied yams with marshmallows, cranberry sauce out of can and the strangest delicacy of American culture, the Jell-O salad (I've tasted my last Jell-O salad).

Tradition Improved

For families big on tradition, I've provided my Tradition Improved holiday meal. It'll satisfy the old guard and enlighten the others to a refreshing improvement.

I hold true to the stuffed bird, but replace the big turkey with a set of stuffed game hens. These small birds are juicy and full of flavor. They're also small enough to serve in halves or whole, so everyone gets to enjoy the variety of different parts from thigh to breast and isn't stuck with two big slices of white meat. For the

And you can figure that if her family is pleased with you, she will be pleased. You could get lucky again.

dressing, we'll start with a boxed stuffing and add a few steps to enhance the flavor from bland to perfection.

Let's begin with some shrimp with a tomatillo and cilantro broth. I've found that even traditionalists are open to different ideas for holiday appetizers. This dish is unusual but delicious and will be a welcome twist.

Re-Stuffed Russets give a flavorful alternative to the holiday staple mashed potatoes. Match them up with a Watercress & Duck Salad to provide a little roughage with the spread. It's a unique salad mixing duck with watercress, which has an inherent spicy taste. Seasonal nuts and a citrus flair round out the dish.

Tradition Removed

If your guests are looking for something different, then the Tradition Removed menu will do. We replace the bird with a prime rib-eye. Beef is always a man's favorite. For this delectable cut, we trim the fat, coat the meat with flavorful rosemary and then serve with a spicy horseradish sauce. It's very easy to prepare, which allows you to attend to the other dishes.

Baked Alaska is a whole salmon served with a mustard dill sauce. This is a wonderful buffet item, but works well as an appetizer at the table, too. It is one of the easiest dishes to cook, yet it will impress all of your guests when they see it on the table.

I complement the main dishes with Italian Stallion Penne, which adds a little Italian flair to the holiday dinner. (Hey, I'm a product of my upbringing.) The sauce's flavor comes from the sausage, so put some effort into getting good ones. The Macho Grill is a vegetable dish for varied tastes. Even non-veggie eaters find this squash dish tasty.

If you are hosting family and friends who really like to eat and you need additional dishes, the recipes in Her Bunco Night and The Weekend Pass are designed for events similar to holidays. They're not only complementary, but a perfect fit for most holiday functions.

So enjoy working in the kitchen and leave 'em guessing about your sexuality. That always makes for good table conversation.

Happy holidays!

TRADITION IMPROVED

Hors d'oeuvres

Tomatillo Shrimp
Fresh shrimp served in a thick spicy cilantro broth

Salad

Watercress & Duck
*Roasted duck tossed in a watercress salad with pine nuts
in an orange vinaigrette*

Main Courses

Game Hen
Oven-roasted Cornish game hen stuffed with a chicken gizzard dressing

Leg of Pork
Oven roasted pork leg

Vegetables

Re-Stuffed Russets
Twice-baked potatoes with sour cream and chives

Dessert

Traditional dish to be provided by the eldest female guest

TOMATILLO SHRIMP

INGREDIENTS

Medium raw shrimp .2 pounds (peeled/deveined)

Onion. . . . . 1 medium

Jalapeno/serrano peppers 4

Lemon 1

Parsley . . . . .1 cup

Tomatillos . . . . .2 cups

Cilantro . . . . .1 cup

Chicken broth. . . . . .1 cup

Olive oil . . . . 3 tablespoons

Step one

- Remove leaves of cilantro and parsley from stems
- Chop onion and tomatillos into 1/4" squares
- Mince jalapenos

Step two

- Preheat olive oil in a large pan
- Add onions, tomatillos, peppers and cook over medium heat for 5 minutes
- Remove from heat and let stand for 5 minutes

Step three

- While mixture is cooling, bring water to boil in large saucepan
- Add shrimp and lemon (cut in half and squeezed) and cook for approximately 3 minutes or until shrimp turns white

Step four

- Pour tomatillo mixture into blender, and add cilantro, parsley and chicken broth
- Blend for 10 –15 seconds
- Return mixture to pan and reheat

Step five

- Drain shrimp
- Toss into tomatillo sauce and serve

Serves 6 – 8

WATERCRESS & DUCK

INGREDIENTS

Watercress . . . . 1 bunch

Duck legs* 2

Pine nuts . . . . 2 oz. (¼ cup)

Orange . . . . ½

Orange Vinaigrette:

Olive oil . . . . 2 tablespoons

White wine vinegar . . . . 1 tablespoon

Juice from orange . . . . 1 tablespoon

Step one

- Preheat oven and roast duck legs at 350° for 1 hour
- When done remove skin
- Slice duck into 1/4" by 1" strips

Step two

Prepare orange vinaigrette

- In small cup mix 2 tablespoons each of olive oil and orange juice, and 1 tablespoon of white wine vinegar

Step three

- Chop watercress 3/4" lengths
- Combine duck, pine nuts and watercress in salad bowl
- Add orange vinaigrette, toss and serve

Serves 2

Hearty portion

- For holiday serving use whole duck and multiply other ingredients by four

Serves up to 12

*Note –
If duck legs are unavailable, use whole duck and allow extra hour cooking time

GAME HEN

HOW TO MAKE GAME HEN

INGREDIENTS

Games hens	6
Onion	1 large
Celery	4 stalks
Stuffing mix	12 oz. box
Chicken hearts and gizzards	1 lb.
Butter	2 oz. (¼ cup)
Olive oil	2 tablespoons

Step one
- Add the root end and the top leaves of celery along with 1/2 onion to pot of water
- Remove parts from game hens, combine with chicken hearts and gizzards, add to pot and boil for 1 hour

Step two
- Discard celery, onions and necks from pot
- Remove remaining chicken parts (gizzards, hearts and livers) and mince into 1/4" squares
- Save liquid stock from pot

Step three
- Chop remaining 1/2 of raw onion and equal amount of raw celery in 1/4" squares
- Heat large pan and add 2 tablespoons of olive oil, 2 ounces of butter, onions, celery and minced chicken parts
- Cook for approximately 5 minutes, stirring occasionally
- Add stuffing mix and enough stock to moisten stuffing

Step four
- Remove stuffing from heat
- Stuff cavities of each hen

Step five
- Preheat oven to 450° and cook hens for 1½ – 2 hours
- Occasionally brush hens with butter to brown

Serves 6 – 12

LEG OF PORK

INGREDIENTS

Pork leg . . . . 10 – 20 lbs.

Parsley . . . . .1 bunch

Step one

- Preheat oven to 350°
- Place leg on a rack in a deep roasting pan and put in oven. Cook time is approximately 20 minutes per pound (A rack is convenient but not necessary)
- If you have a meat thermometer, insert in thickest part of thigh. Pork leg is done when internal temperature is 160 – 170°

Step two

- Remove leg from oven
- Place on serving platter and cover with foil until ready to serve

Serves 8 – 12

RE-STUFFED RUSSETS

INGREDIENTS

Russet potatoes	18 small
Sour cream	1 cup
Chives	½ cup
Butter	1 cube (¼ lb.)
Milk	1 cup

Step one

- Poke small hole in each potato with sharp knife and place in preheated oven at 425° degrees for approximately 1 hour
- When done remove potatoes from oven, let cool for 10 minutes and cut potatoes in half lengthwise

Step two

- Scoop out potato from skins and put into large bowl
- Save skins from 12 potatoes

Step three

- Chop chives in 1/8" squares

Step four

- Mash potatoes. Add butter, sour cream, milk and chives
- Salt and pepper to taste
- Mix well

Step five

- Add mashed potatoes back into potato skins
- Return to oven for 15 minutes at 500° before serving

24 servings

More or less milk should be used to get the desired consistency.

TRADITION REMOVED

156

Hors d'oeuvres

Baked Alaska
Whole salmon oven-baked and served with parsley-mustard dipping sauce

Salad

Apple Endive
*Endive, diced apple, crumbled blue cheese, chopped walnuts
and an accent of Dijon*

Main Courses

Prime Rib-Eye
Oven-roasted prime rib served with creamed horseradish

Italian Stallion Penne
*Fire-roasted Italian sausages simmered in a tomato sauce
served over a bed of pasta*

Vegetables

Macho Grill
Grilled acorn squash, pasilla peppers and onions

Dessert

To be provided by the eldest male guest

BAKED ALASKA

INGREDIENTS

Whole salmon	4 – 6 lbs.
Sour cream	1 cup
Dijon mustard	2 oz. (¼ cup)
Parsley	6 sprigs
Lemons	4
Olive oil	2 – 3 tablespoons

Step one

- Preheat oven to 450°
- Wipe cookie sheet with thin layer of olive oil, add whole salmon and place in oven
- Cook for 40 minutes until center of thickest portion is slightly rare

Step two

- While salmon is cooking, in a bowl prepare sauce by combining minced parsley, mustard, sour cream and 4 tablespoons of juice from 1 lemon

Step three

- Transfer salmon to serving platter
- Gently remove skin from top half of salmon
- Garnish with remaining lemons and parsley and serve with dipping sauce

When top half has been eaten by guests, gently remove bone and continue to enjoy.

Step one hint
To test if the salmon is done, enter through the underbelly so you don't damage the skin for presentation.

APPLE ENDIVE

INGREDIENTS

Endive	1 head
Walnuts (chopped)	2 oz.
Blue cheese (crumbled)	2 oz.
Dijon mustard	2 tablespoons
Lime	1
Apple	1 medium
Olive oil	8 tablespoons

Step one

- Slice endive leaves in 3/4" pieces
- Cut apple, remove seeds and chop into 1/4" squares

Step two

- In a large bowl, mix apple, Dijon mustard, walnuts, olive oil, blue cheese and juice from lime (2 tablespoons)

Step three

- Add endive on top of mixture
- Cover with plastic wrap and place in refrigerator

Step four

- Toss ingredients just before serving

Serves 6 – 8

Storing the salad without mixing in the dressing preserves the crispness of the endive.

PRIME RIB EYE

INGREDIENTS

Rosemary . . . . 6 sprigs

Prime rib . . . . 5 lbs.

Sour cream . . . . 8 oz. (1 cup)

Pure horseradish . . . . 2 oz. (¼ cup)

Step one

- Trim excess fat from roast
- Separate rosemary leaves from stems
- Finely chop leaves

Step two

- Preheat oven at 425°
- Place roast in a large roasting pan, salt and pepper
- Spread rosemary evenly over roast. Pat with hands to help adhere to roast

Step three

- Cook approximately 1½ hours until medium rare in the middle

Tip

A meat thermometer takes away the risk of overcooking.

Step four

- Combine horseradish and sour cream in small bowl. Mix well and store in the refrigerator until needed

Step five

- When roast is done remove from oven and cover with aluminum foil until ready to serve (Don't wait too long!)

Serves 6 – 8

1

2

Rack is useful, but not necessary.

ITALIAN STALLION PENNE

INGREDIENTS

Italian sausage, ...12

Tomatoes . . . . .6 medium

Onion. .1 medium

Basil . . . . 10 sprigs

Penne pasta . . . . 1½ lbs. Uncooked

Vegetable broth. . . . . 3 cups

Olive oil . . . . .4 tablespoons

Step one

- Brown Italian sausage in pan or grill on barbeque (Approximately 10 – 15 minutes)

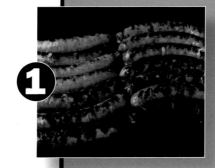

Step two

- Chop onions and tomatoes into 3/8" cubes
- Preheat 2 tablespoons of olive oil in pot
- Add onions and cook over medium heat for approximately 4 minutes
- Add sausage, tomatoes and vegetable broth to pot
- Simmer for 1 hour

Step three

- Approximately 20 minutes before sausage is done boil water in large pot
- Add 2 tablespoons each of salt and olive oil to 5 quarts of water
- After water is boiling, add penne pasta and cook until done, approximately 10 minutes

Step four

- Remove sausage and place on platter
- Chop basil

Step five

- Take sauce remaining from cooking sausage and put in blender. Blend for 5 – 10 seconds
- Pour half of the sauce over penne and lightly toss so pasta doesn't stick
- Place penne, remaining sauce and sausage in separate bowls
- Garnish penne with chopped basil

Serves 9 – 12

MACHO GRILL

INGREDIENTS

Onion	1 medium
Acorn squash	1
Pasila peppers	2
Olive oil	1 - 2 tablespoons
Butter	1 - 2 tablespoons

Step one

- Peel squash, cut in half and remove seeds
- Peel onion
- Cut peppers in half, remove seeds and stems

Step two

- Cut squash, onions and peppers into 1/2" squares
- Combine in bowl with approximately 2 parts squash to 1 part onions and 1 part peppers

Step three

- Preheat 1 tablespoon each of olive oil and butter to a non-stick pan over medium heat
- Add squash, onions and peppers and cook over medium heat until squash is done, turning periodically to brown all sides while adding salt and pepper to taste (approximately 20 minutes)

Serves 4 – 6

Variation
Pasilla peppers vary in taste from mild to medium hot and are best suited. If the only peppers available are other mild green chilies or green bell peppers, use them, but add a very finely chopped jalapeno.

POST GAME NOTES

Thank you
Stephens Press, LLC.
and Visual Impact, Inc.
Great job!

Dinner at Her Place...
The Cheat Sheet

Unlike playing in the NFL, there's some definite advantages to playing an away game in the dating world. Put it this way, when you've been invited over for dinner at her place, you crossed midfield while walking up to her door. If she's allowing you to cook in her kitchen, you're in the Red Zone. You can't afford a turnover here.

This is a pressure situation. You can't take your playbook onto the field. The defense will be onto that. And unfortunately, unless you're wearing long sleeves, you can't put it on a wristband either. As funny as that would be for the rest of us guys, I'm not sure she'd get the humor. So, as your coach from the sidelines, I've provided you with a choice of touchdown recipes from The Date chapter on business card size 'Cheat Sheets' for you to reference.

Still prepare by studying this book with the step-by-step photography, but have the card of the dish your preparing in your wallet. You don't want to miss a step, and you don't want to show your hand. You've told her you can cook so she can't see you reading recipes. You'd blow the vision.

All tips, photos, and variations have been removed in order to fit this inconspicuously in your wallet, therefore, study the plays before game time. The sheet is designed so that we don't miss a critical block or passing route while in the Red Zone.

Tip — If it's me, and she's not provided me any space in the kitchen, then I'd ask, "Excuse me, where's your bathroom?" Make my way down the hall. Lock the door. Pull out the card for a quick review. Hit the flush. Wash my hands and I'm back in control. That comes from experience.

Now note that none of the salads are in the cheat sheets. We've only got so much space to work with and they're easier to remember, plus you can prepare most of them in advance.

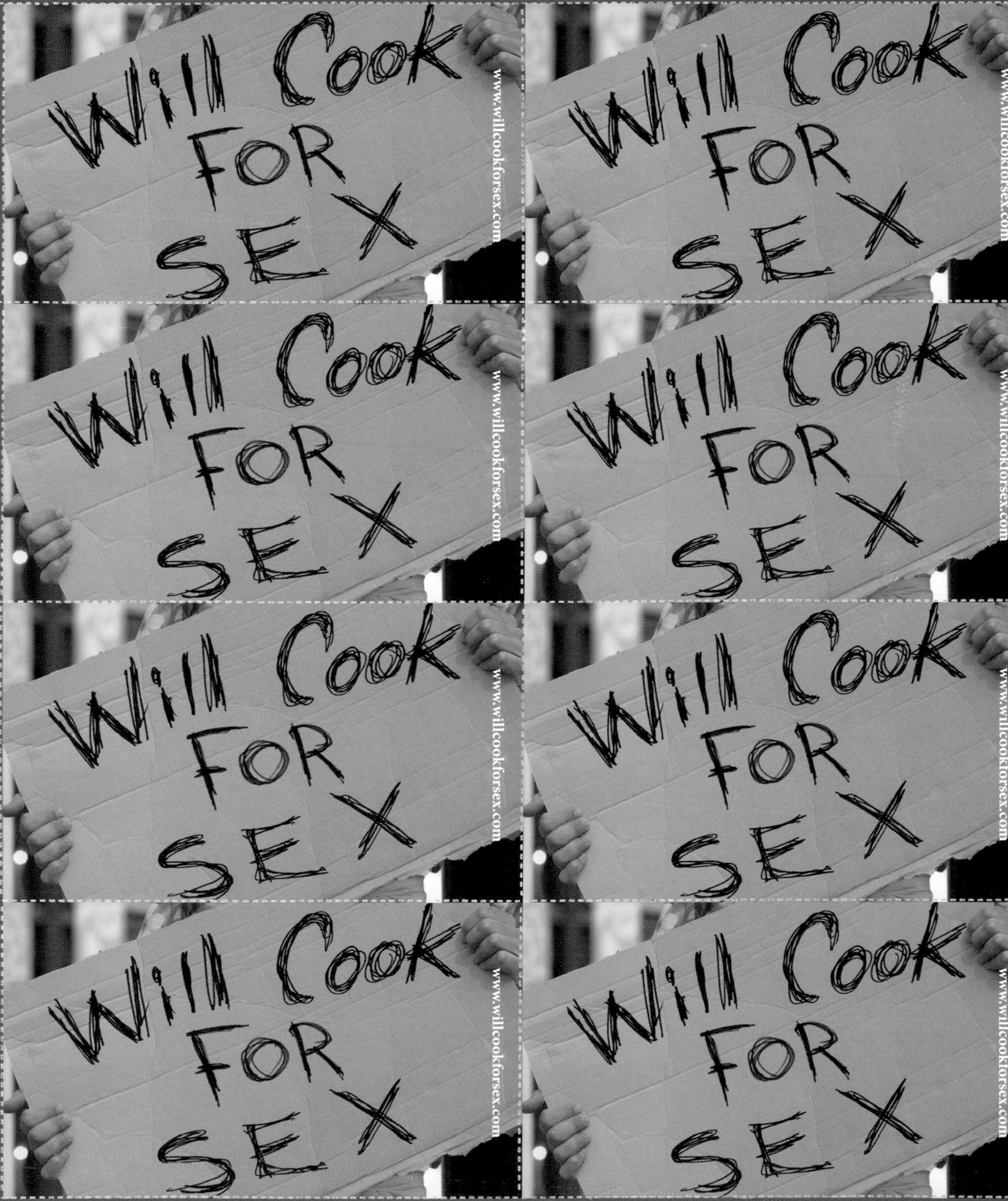
Will Cook
FOR
SEX
www.willcookforsex.com

POWER PLAY PUCKS

Ingredients:
Mango ... 1
Scallops ... 6 large
Parsley ... 2 sprigs
Milk ... 3 tablespoons
Cayenne pepper ... Dash
Olive oil ... ½ teaspoon

Step one:
• Peel and slice the mango. Discard the seed and skin.
• Add mango, splash of milk and dash of cayenne pepper to blender and puree the mixture.

Step two:
• Preheat med sized non-stick pan, add a few drops of olive oil
• Brown scallops on both sides over med/high heat
• Cooking time for the scallops is about 2-3 minutes on each side

Step three:
• Place mango puree on plate — Best at room temperature
• Add the scallops on top of the puree
• Garnish with parsley

SEAHAWK PASTA

Ingredients:
Avocado ... 1 large
Farfalle (bowtie shaped pasta) ... 6 oz.
Vegetable broth ... 1½ cups
Shallot ... 1
Salmon fillet ... ¾ – 1 lb.
Olive oil ... 2 tablespoons
Flour ... 1 tablespoon

Step one:
• Bring 1 quart of water to boil with 1 tablespoon each of salt and olive oil

Step two:
• Slice the salmon in approximately 1/2" squares
• Cut avocado into approximately 1/2" squares
• Mince (chop finely) the shallots

Step three:
• Add pasta to boiling water for approximately 8 – 10 minutes. Do not overcook

Step four:
• Preheat 1 tablespoon of olive oil in pan
• Add minced shallot and cook over medium heat for approximately 2 minutes

Step five:
• Add salmon to pan
• Lightly cook for 1 – 2 minutes
• While the salmon is cooking, sprinkle a teaspoon of flour over the salmon

Step six:
• Add vegetable broth slowly to salmon and as contents begin to boil, reduce heat.
• Salt and pepper to taste
• Add a dash white or cayenne pepper should you want it spicy

Step seven:
• Add cooked pasta, stir and then gently fold in avocado squares

LOBSTER SPEARS

Ingredients:
Raw lobster tails ... 8 oz – 10 oz.
Parsley ... 6 sprigs
Belgian endive ... 2 stalks
Avocado ... 1
Chives (fresh) ... 12 strands
Mayonnaise ... 2 tablespoons

Step one:
• Slice open lobster from underneath tail and remove meat
• Cut into 3/8" squares
• Slice avocado into thin 1/8" strips
• Mince (chop finely) chives

Step two:
• Preheat 2 tablespoons of olive oil in pan
• Add lobster and cook over medium heat for approximately four minutes, stirring occasionally
• Let cool and place in small bowl
• Add mayonnaise and mix
• Salt and pepper to taste

Step three:
• Remove twelve leaves from endive stalks
• Place 1 slice of avocado in each leaf
• Add a small portion of lobster mix on top of avocado
• Sprinkle minced chives on top of each spear
• Garnish with parsley and serve

SWAMP WATER SEA BASS

Ingredients:
Chilean sea bass ... ½ lb.
Watercress ... 4 sprigs
Curry powder ... 1 tablespoon
Butter lettuce ... 2 leaves
Milk or half & half ... ¼ cup
Vegetable stock ... 1 cup

Step one:
• Place lettuce, watercress, curry powder, vegetable stock and milk in blender
• Add mixture to small/medium pan

Step two:
• Add sea bass filets
• Over medium/high heat poach fish until done (approximately 3 minutes)

Step three:
• Transfer sea bass to medium sized flat soup bowl
• Add curry sauce just enough not to cover the sea bass
• Garnish with watercress sprigs

RED ZONE CHOPS

Ingredients:
Lamb chops ... 4
Rosemary ... 4 stems
Cracked pepper ... 2 tablespoons

Step one:
• Remove rosemary leaves from stem
• Chop leaves finely

Step two:
• Trim fat from lamb chops (optional)
• Sprinkle pepper on both sides of lamb chops
• Generously add rosemary on top of pepper and pat lightly with hand to help adhere to chops

Step three:
• Pre-heat grill on high
• Place chops on grill
• Approximately 2 – 3 minutes per side

Step four:
• Place chops on plate, garnish with parsley

BLUE COLLAR SOUFFLÉ

Ingredients:
Butter (unsalted) ... 4 tablespoons
Eggs ... 2 large eggs
Sugar ... 4 tablespoons
Bittersweet chocolate ... 4 oz.
Flour ... 2½ tablespoons
Vanilla ice cream ... 2 scoops

Step one:
• Preheat oven to 400°. Put chocolate and butter in a double boiler over low heat and stir until chocolate is melted. (A mixing bowl on top of a sauce pan with a cup of water can be used in place of a double boiler.)

Step two:
• In a small bowl or cup mix sugar and flour

Step three:
• In a medium bowl, whisk eggs, then whisk in flour and sugar.

Step four:
• Whisk in chocolate into egg mixture

Step five:
• Scrape mixture into two 1 cup baking bowls (glass or ceramic called ramekins) and bake for approximately 15 minutes until edges are firm and center is still soft

Step six:
• Add scoop of vanilla ice cream to center and serve immediately

BREAKAWAY SHANKS

Ingredients:
Veal shanks ... 4
Egg noodles ... 8 oz.
Fresh basil ... 4-6 sprigs
Onion ... 1
Chicken broth ... 2 cups
Tomatoes ... 4 medium
Flour ... ¼ cup
Olive oil ... 3 tablespoons

Step one:
• Chop (dice) onions into 1/2" squares
• Flour veal shanks

Step two:
• Preheat (1) tablespoon of olive oil in pan and pot
• Add onions to pan and cook over medium heat for approximately 4 minutes
• Add veal shanks to pot and brown on both sides

Step three:
• Add sautéed onions, tomatoes cut in 1/2" squares and chicken broth to veal shanks
• Bring to boil, lower heat and simmer until shanks are tender. (Approximately 2½ – 3 hours)

Step four:
• About 15 minutes before serving bring two quarts of water to boil with 1 tablespoon each of salt and olive oil
• Add noodles to boiling water 6 – 8 minutes

Step five:
• Remove shanks from pot
• Transfer liquid to blender and blend
• Salt and pepper to taste
• Remove from blender and add to noodles

Step five:
• Place noodles on plate
• Put veal shanks in center
• Slice basil leaves, top each plate and serve

DERBY DAY SALMON

Ingredients:
Parsley or watercress leaves ... 1 tablespoon
Salmon steaks ... 2
Fresh grated horseradish root ... ¼ cup
Cucumber (peeled, seeded & sliced) ... ½
Breadcrumbs ... ¼ cup
Sour cream ... ¼ cup
Mayonnaise ... 3 tablespoons

Step one:
• Peel and grate horseradish root

Step two:
• In a small bowl mix horseradish, bread crumbs and mayonnaise
• Salt and pepper to taste
• Mix well and store in the refrigerator until needed

Step three:
• Place salmon steaks on a lightly oiled baking sheet
• Spread horseradish mixture evenly over fish on top side
• Preheat oven to 450°

Step four:
• Bake filets for 10 – 12 minutes until fish is resilient when pressed at the thickest part

Step five:
• Place cucumber, sour cream and parsley (or watercress) in a blender
• Salt and pepper to taste
• Transfer sauce to small pan and warm over low heat

Step six:
• Place sauce on plate
• Place salmon on top
• Garnish and serve